Mesopotopia

BOOKS, CHAPBOOKS, AND COLLABORATIONS
BY ANNE WALDMAN

On the Wing

O My Life!

Up Through the Years

Giant Night

Baby Breakdown

Memorial Day
(with Ted Berrigan)

Icy Rose

No Hassles

Holy City

Light & Shadow

Spin Off

The West Indies Poems

Life Notes: Selected Poems

Self Portrait (with Joe
Brainard)

The Contemplative Life

Fast Speaking Woman

Sun the Blonde Out

The Basketball Article
(with Bernadette Mayer)

*Fast Speaking Woman and
Other Chants*

Journals & Dreams

Hotel Room

Shaman/Shamane

Sphinxeries
(with Denyse Du Roi)

Four Travels (with Reed Bye)

To a Young Poet

Polar Ode (with Eileen Myles)

Countries (with Reed Bye)

Cabin

First Baby Poems

Makeup on Empty Space

Invention (with Susan Hall)

Den Mond in Farbe Sehen

Skin Meat Bones

Blue Mosque

The Romance Thing

*Tell Me About It: Poems for
Painters*

*Helping the Dreamer: New &
Selected Poems, 1966–1988*

Her Story
(with Elizabeth Murray)

Not a Male Pseudonym

Lokapala

Fait Accompli

Troubairitz

Iovis: All Is Full of Jove

Kill or Cure

Homage to Allen G.
(with George Schneeman)

Iovis II

Kin (with Susan Rothenberg)

Polemics (with Anselm Hollo
& Jack Collom)

Donna Che Parla Veloce

Young Manhattan
(with Bill Berkson)

One Voice in Four Parts
(with Richard Tuttle)

Marriage: A Sentence

Au Lit/Holy (with Eleni
Sikelianos & Laird Hunt)

*Vow to Poetry: Essays,
Interviews, & Manifestos*

War Crime

[Things] Seen Unseen

*Dark Arcana / Afterimage or
Glow*

*In the Room of Never Grieve:
New & Selected Poems, 1985–
2003*

Zombie Dawn
(with Tom Clark)

*Structure of the World
Compared to a Bubble*

Beat Roots
(with George Schneeman)

Outrider

Femme Qui Parle Vite

Red Noir

Nine Nights Meditation
(with Donna Dennis)

Martyrdom

Manatee/Humanity

Matriot Acts

Soldatesque/Soldiering
(with Noah Saterstrom)

*The Iovis Trilogy: Colors in the
Mechanism of Concealment*

Cry Stall Gaze (with Pat Steir)

Gossamurmur

*Archives, Pour Un Monde
Menacé*

Aubaderrying
(with Mimi Gross)

Jaguar Harmonics

*Sweet-Voiced [Mutilated]
Papyrus* (with Pamela Lawton)

*Voice's Daughter of a Heart Yet
to Be Born*

Empty Set (with Alexis Myre)

Fantastic Caryatids
(with Vincent Katz)

Extinction Aria

Trickster Feminism

Mundo Aparte / Offworld

Sanctuary

*all rainbows in a brainstem that
we be so contained*
(with Nathlie Provosty)

Goslings to Prophecy
(with Emma Gomis)

A Punch in the Gut of a Star
(with Emma Gomis)

*Become a Midnight Star / para
ser Estrella a medianoche*

Bard, Kinetic

Shortest Century
(with Zoe Brezsny)

Pecados Para Tragar Cohetes

Rues du Monde

The Velvet Wire
(with No Land)

Tendrel

Archivist Scissors

13 Moons Kora

Quantum's Wing
(with Douglas Dunn)

Mesopotopia

Anne Waldman

PENGUIN POETS

PENGUIN BOOKS
An imprint of Penguin Random House LLC
1745 Broadway, New York, NY 10019
penguinrandomhouse.com

Set in 12/15 Fournier MT Pro
Designed by Sabrina Bowers

LIBRARY OF CONGRESS CATALOGING-IN-PUBLICATION DATA
Names: Waldman, Anne, 1945– author.
Title: Mesopotopia / Anne Waldman.
Description: New York, NY : Penguin Books, 2025. | Includes bibliographical references.
Identifiers: LCCN 2025017062 (print) | LCCN 2025017063 (ebook) |
ISBN 9780143137023 (trade paperback) | ISBN 9780525508540 (ebook)
Subjects: LCGFT: Poetry.
Classification: LCC PS3573.A4215 M47 2025 (print) |
LCC PS3573.A4215 (ebook) | DDC 811/.54—dc23/eng/20250424
LC record available at https://lccn.loc.gov/2025017062
LC ebook record available at https://lccn.loc.gov/2025017063

Printed in the United States of America
1st Printing

The authorized representative in the EU for product safety and compliance is Penguin Random House Ireland, Morrison Chambers, 32 Nassau Street, Dublin D02 YH68, Ireland, https://eu-contact.penguin.ie.

for Mei-mei Berssenbrugge

The field of heaven, which operates outside space-time, is formed
by acts of other entities, other stars, and by people who rise in the
dark to look for them and place them.

from Mei-mei Berssenbrugge's *A Treatise on Stars*

Who are we, us the children of History, whose, which period, what side of History, the wars or the poems, the queens or the strangers, on which side of whose History are we going to be? Are we going to be?

—Etel Adnan, *There*

Randa Sammour: Where is a safe area? There is no safety. Where is safety? We flee every day. We get displaced every day under the rockets, under the bombing. I am alone with my little children. I flee with them every day from a place to another. I don't know where to go. They tell you about safe areas. Where is safety? Make me feel safe. Make the little child feel safe. We are tired, people. It's enough. Have mercy on us.

—from *Democracy Now!*

Acknowledgments

An earlier version of "Nocturne" was published in the spring 2019 issue of Bard College's literary journal, *Conjunctions* (issue 72). I offer gratitude to the editor, Bradford Morrow.

"Nocturne," also in an earlier version, appeared in the Louisiana Literary Festival Museum edition, Denmark, 2019.

"Nocturne: Martyrdom," in an earlier version as "Martyrdom," was printed in a chaplet published by Palm Press, Los Angeles, 2009.

"Parables," "Blood Moon," "Blue Moons' Omens," and "Avicennan Medicine" were first published in *Peripheries: A Journal of Word, Image, and Sound*, by Harvard University Press, 2021.

An earlier version of "Extinction Aria, Its Exegesis, the Realms" was published by David Sellers and Pied Oxen Printers in 2017. Images are used by permission of publisher, printer, and designer.

"Sins to Swallow Rockets" was previously published as "Pecados Para Tragar Cohetes" by *El Leopardo de las Nieves*, translated by Lucía Hinojosa Gaxiola, Mexico, 2022.

The epigraph in "Curandera" is commonly attributed to Brice Marden.

Thanks to the New York Public Library for their study rooms and special collections.

Thanks to Zoe Brezsny for her poetry, intuitive gnosis, and friendship.

Thanks to Amy Rupert for thoughtful conversation and manuscript preparation.

Heartfelt gratitude to all those who helped in existing: Chris Maher, Reed Bye, Jill Jones, Vincent Katz, Diana Lizette Rodriguez, Pat Steir, Devin Brahja Waldman, Ambrose Bye, Kora Bye Anaya, Natalia Gaia, Alystyre Julian, Patti Smith, Jeffery Pethybridge, Swanee Astrid, Georgia Wartel Collins, Alice Notley, Douglas Dunn, Jennifer Firestone, Lee Anne Brown, Althea Abruscato, Luna Luz, Nic Abruscato, Sarah Riggs, Meredith Monk, Peter Hale, Erika Hodges, Martina Salisbury, Bob Holman, the T. S. Eliot Foundation, and dearest beloved Ed Bowes.

Thanks to David Kermani for the use of the John Ashbery collage and for some lines from John's poem *Flow Chart*.

Thanks to Paul Slovak, Allie Merola, Sonia Gadre, and the Penguin Books team for the inspired edits, design, and production of this manuscript.

Sky in Gaze

did you / did you / the brindled rivers entwined / did you see / did
you see / devotees / archangels / poetry / horses / planets up there /
okay, I'll look / an *Apatosaurus louisae* / *I'll look up or way down under*
/ did you frame and reckon? / *reckon what?* / an alphabet / was it
in flames? / *yes* / did it tremble? / *yes* / did you see? / *o yes, vortex*
/ golden letters / beckoning, auras, like saints like troubadours? /
singing / did the top of your head open / nectar come down / was there
song? / angels singing / was it diving within / when you were small
/ commanding / take me up / rise up / asking / did the sky / did that
sky / rise you up? / like a volcano / did you call out? / rising you up,
dizzy / call back? / levitate? / did it call? / did it quake? / with naming
of origins?

Contents

Mesopotopia

Herminuisance: Mesopotopia the Intro

This world age was supposed to have been candles & canticles & invention & amulets, and intervention & romance & wit & civilization & mantras of nonsense & bright destiny & the epic plan become essential desire, voice, vow. And through ages ritual to sink your heart into to raise you up from endurance. And time your trouble time was supposed to be your elevation your apotheosis all the forms of poetry making and your feet dance in the tread and the history of spirit, and threads of open systems and working to make it through many hours of night. Memorizing, placing the word, the lune, the loom the song & humming of the bird once more back into your heart, human. Your strophes & twists & turnings, human. Asleep on the wing, all the merry "mancys"—geomancy and what is the origin of this suffix? And what is your origin in the bright naked day dark of the night?

And existence, the continuum from how it begins. Antsy. The Animal. Human. No clue. But war.

A Marxist Berber St. Augustine confessing his passion in astrology before conversion? "I hoped to attack and refute and make a laughing-stock of the demented people who make a living by astrology." O Lordy.

Dawn song & lover leaving to meditate down Second Avenue, in an old scriptorium. And doing this becomes ritual, and a prophecy to stave off death. And the library you are making are the documents of sacred time. Are fear & paranoia allowed in the documents of your sacred time in the Free University Library? Documents to live by, hide by, blueprints for how to become all the genders and how to become all the lovers, how to be care & empathy in the sacred library of genders & lovers. To what you least expected, nowhere to hide now. Here is your card, here is your golden card for the golden library of words. For the Armory show of words & books in the reckoning. Here is the inventory. Read up. A race against time because we are in the speed zones now. And I'm just coasting down Avenue A.

All the staves, uplifted scaffold in verses in the construction of a tower working herculean to build and come down again and build again. Come down from your perch is over. Come down it is quaking, all stones & tones of origin. Cruising.

But there is nothing in the multiuniverse or in space this realm of what is and is not that is not making consciousness, quaking in consciousness, making rounds of consciousness. We continue the cyclidic, armed for beauty & love. New countenance. Coup d'état.

The Syriac round dance of martyrs and other prophets, witches, warriors is choreographed before you are born. May being around dance of poetry & prophets & witches & warriors & voyants & valence find release.

> Remnants of prophecy.
> Speak in tongues polarity
> In archaic forms
> Who understands possession? a voice orchestrated with organs
>   slung in the body?
>
> Tell more of my Genesis, my ribs my sins
>
> Tell me Tibetan Marpa, the translator, the traveler
>
> Milarepa the poet, skin turns green eating nettles in a cave
>
> Enkidu, a mere kiddo
>
> Herminuisance the newest guide, jumps in time, old time religion
>
> Goddess scholar Enheduanna, shining through all the rage of a
>   dark age, born 2286 BC.

Thriving in the Mesopotamian renaissance of acumen, poetry,
    weapons rising out of Ishtar's shoulders
Therigatha of mendicant poet-nuns everywhere in a back corridor
Or Aztec tale of the
bound girl
struggled to mark herself with black/white substances in the ancient
    way
waiting in line stood and screamed "Why do you not sacrifice me?"
    Later the bards would report
tears down her face as flames rose up around Shield Flower. *I go to
    where my god lives.*
My people's descendants will all become great warriors, you will see . . .

India
Bauls still dancing in the streets
Gassire, castanets
You will see
Maya: illusion always a dance
Nine shaman songs of woe's men, Eurasian steppes
Ainu to shift
Arabic
Uighur

And now also, is dirge, archival, what we love most lives inside vaults and
waves ripe for evanescence, a particular destruction device locked in the
toolbox. Or antimatter's revenge?

Start over: you will see
It would be the hermit and the dove again arise
It would disavow the nuclear option under rigid scrutiny
The sects & pacts of great inter-species sadly now broken, ebbing.
Plutonium pits again arise, but let's try abandonment of stagecraft.
Let's do it, let's do it, heh! Let's try.

It was to have been a compendium to perform with you, in your ear, in your chariot, a nearby vehicle. You could not succeed in these forms: option, scrutiny, performance of chariots. Way past that. An obsolete vehicle. All spokes gone. It was supposed to have been trumpeted from the earliest time, names, scale of tribes, discoveries of first touch, bone instruments, rattles of teeth, the runes on maps to find a psyche's way back. And as he divined the entheogen I know I had been there before. In the mud, in the long string of the lithe creatures, helping a child grow. Apotheosis.

Shape-shifting Kundry. Licking her toad. "Been there," the toad said. The legend said there were allies "in advance toward ecofeminism."

It would rise to structure, maybe by joining hands and singing in a circle-round, vast in temple ceremony & pomp in a claustrophobic cavern. Back to original texts and urns, Nahuatl annals speak of Ilancueitl, Elder Woman Skirt who allowed the wandering Aztecs to settle in her small town. Not the best idea . . . But it would verify, clarify, mystify the strangers who did not know their code, their mores. This is a parable of old forms.

Then desires of song chant in obedience to the forms of spirit. What are they? Obsolete or advanced? They were supposed to help us guide me to you to be not the dactyls & spondees of war cry, not the blood on the shield but liberation through an act of runes and studying ruins.

Facing your own mirror: lament the master plan, smash it, a generative zone heard the same wistful rift. Break now. And it takes years to master the art of memory.

It was supposed to be a bundle of sticks gathered one at a time or when
   you might need fire
It was supposed to have been Antediluvian energies
Pyramid Funerary texts howling as Pharaohs' eyes and mouths are cut
   open to breathe
Or Subterranean, studying old litmus tests of empire
Ligaments, fur, warmer clothes, graffiti
Testo junkies and sleep shifters, learning the craft
It has to have been a litany, who sang it? For the cradle & birth of
   civilizations
A more minor key. A chorus of saints and newborns
And studying of bhakti saints
Sumerian, Ugaritic, Hittite persons. Who wanted and worshipped
   origins and the end-time. No middle way
Pre-Christian anthologies of struggle & alliance trying to make the
   case, how would you ever know?
What was it? Piling up inside. Learning to be an emotion. Studying to
   be an open-system-singer
Living on borrowed time in claustrophobic echoing hells
For this book is a round
Why is hell to pay?
How far we've come.
This book is a round of systems.

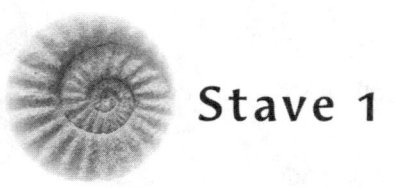

Stave 1

No new transmissions continued. / But we gathered together. / Because closer to the end of the world? / or / new horoscope of "world"—? / Everyone thinks life will end in our lifetime, we are the last / A lucky auspice, a new session / how to become invisible under surveillance / We studied a tricky throne meditation including machinery, and crystalline "messengers" / who hop into gear to translate and mimic weather and then everybody thinks you are high honcho / they can do that, smoke & mirrors / concerned with cinematics of planets in distress, / a prison break, guided hallucination / or cosmic chords or healing or more practical stuff / The bat temple taught us / better, learning to live close with others hanging upside down in the astral omens / already shooting by a century ago YOU MUST be kind / study stoically acts of divination, hoping answers come but you are vehicle-ready / And others have their purpose and you have to go back to the moon landing all over again / And the techniques you learned in the terminal / down on Wall Street.

"Sad grows the river god as
he oars past us"

Telepathy Cross Wounded Galaxies

From Ajanta, the child misplaced her mask
We named her "Have Been Studying"
She became a monk,
A whole life's ears into "It." Here identifying as moonface
Studying the streets, you said I, poet, was an "orations" all my own,
          a "hermetic-sounding" person. So here's an inventory
Mannahatta & mountain, seeking one another, paths cross in the dream
And Continental Divide, its crack-up, the thrust & transit of neutrinos
District Federale
Covarrubias Street
San Juan
Marrakesh
London's upper light Raj shades
And Java's Kedu Plain
And root matrix:
Mohenjo Daro
&
Varanasi, all the ghats, and Calcutta's cineasts and here, misplace
the brunt of language in the crusty city toward spinal sound
and more lists as she traveled, ubiquitous. In a kind of trance.
So we'll always be a crossroad, they said
in sacrifice to poetry's path of naming as
tangles of language, always to the wrong place often
as we name ourselves after poems, and peoples
back a turn of centuries
A scree of origins displaced
As if in a system of runnels for the next war
no one can understand
But when I knew that to say, we had occasion,
Being in the same activist cell, a troop of us
All concerned about Generation Z
and defining as we speak, we kept on

We might only know in song that occasion
The earth runs dry, stealing away recognition
know only prisons
You'd like to be telepathic in all the caves
you travel, all the
world's languages, be human too
Not the ex machina
I've had a lot on my mind as well
A science of communities that need decisive attention
there, don't stop me from reaching out
Convoys of medicines & water, and plant lore
and digging down
What color dye in the simulacrum body for the next text? For the test
Attestation of hesitation accrues then enacts
A rebuttal
Red or blue? Sculptures in yab-yum frisson when the power gets so
    strong under its lid, and all
Starry, ready to pop, to "kiss me deadly," where the director didn't
    understand elder
Unity about old noise, the bomb in the suitcase, the naked woman on the
    highway,
all at risk in the hissing box, look into the abyss, son et lumière
purposeful plankton, secret nuke power
Tens of thousands of innocent victims
What will survive
come after such Indra of alchemy?
Tell me, bravery, to be myself, your poet, and you Geshe, my first teacher
to read the golden texts we mimeographed to bring "mantra to suburbia"
as my girlfriend Hannah said
Escape, back there, have been studying a boy's limbs
How to play the gong, the strict time of
The slendro, and what to sing about
What we know of Ajanta I visited a new moon ago
The new telepathic were saying this too, "moons ago" audibly
And La Monte was in trance with us all day, dawn songs

How to reach behind a ghost, artificial in a way but young
As ghost could only die once, in a swan-song-simulacrum
"You mean ashes in a fascist enterprise?"
"All malevolent demons or animals beamed up the scale?"
So that's a clutter, getting there? Up a ladder "designed for Satan"?
A lot of talk about Satan, why they ask, the younger students
And the talk in the car last night of "our people"
and she said some great-great-great-ancestor was a certified witch
About how all the religious fanatics were "mad for devils . . ."
something—vampires they were, and hungry as Pinochet
or Cotton Mather . . .
"and like right now, USA 2025" and my informant had kin on both sides
Many women stalked out and the point was to see a devil, or be a devil
a kind of upmanship for women
without attachment
stand in for starlight
that the conjunction you met
at the Atmospheric Research Center knows best
way, to carry you into a devil's bargain
he was all science, a small coat; I love his bifocals
are they real? many questions about our future harmony
impostors of the science on the "remotes" learning days
science's demonology, one last chance, flexing a plague
in a flutter of flitting light
"I am here to release top secrets, the map for the
secret raid that changes the world axis one more time"
a new podcast on plutonium, that old element gone dangerously rotting
that will not meet you ever again in your lifetime, be your mount
of ruminations of mystic hidden treasures, those poet friends but in the books
Assyria, Babylon, all I am telling, they have their old queries too
what animal do you ride? what pedestal are you on? who is sexy in this era?
you'd need a diamond beam to see how to climb really high, and folds in a
    plenum
that was an intervention travel the boy said, something not really spoken of
in India, but the temple problem lies exposed who was abused, sacrificed?

Temples, meant virgins
acculturation of modest passing of planets in night
and do in dreams where he swore it was all mothers riding by
say it's true but all the mothers are there
weeping in sorrow, by the crux of Mohenjo & Daro
What else in a cold hell but ride and weep, Euphrates
and you have never seen such suffering in from channel current from the
    remote view
it devours humanity, o mothers
how can you even write? remotely
after atrocity, walk by Tigris now
of birthplace, deaths, charnel house . . .
and beyond mothers who carry the creative intelligence of angels, astral
    beings, guardians, bodhisattvas
In the room, how could you, the boy in my arms, standing in for all boys,
Not stay curious about the body of time, you share in
And we conjured she, the emphasis was on *inquiry with the mother*
Save the house! Save the wisdom! Save the children
as we called it, a crater really, defenseless immediately
Arms or séance you offer, already hacked
Or table rapping, save your shelter
How to save a center of your existence as a hearth
And you create your own family
Had-Been-Studying reaching the ancestors
Was studying the way war returned, incessantly talk about it
Displacement of the human to what end?
As the white army fuses the Capitol
and you want to migrate to the next imagination
I kept saying "you know the secrets of evolving," of telepathy, dear
    informant!
Trying to address the way we are astride on the catastrophic playground
Tribes & land
Lots brewing a drawdown? Ketamine?
As you'll expose the cage opening to the chaos, the leather straps on the
atom bomb in the prehistoric movie, was a dinosauric explosion

We don't even talk in centuries anymore, we talk in comets
They'll let you out from your black hole for a little breather while
you write your encomium, and children next time
In the last at school desk learning epistles
I wrote to Dr. Schweitzer and got a reply
The civil school time, respecting elders
You could be as me was the gist
and we heard back from wild-haired Dr. Einstein too
You said you'd been studying
Been studying it, in part, how to spring out off local doors
water or the cages at "Abu Ghraib"
Hamptons, Frank's memory of feelings
Here were many doors. Creeley's shot at moment knocking
but one pink rush of de Kooning, another sharp mind
as he lost all but memory of paint & brush
And Kabir said, in his postmod-prophecy
"Men with new art theory will be coming your way through a new door"
Talk about the dead moving through art walls and jumping out
if you conjure them. At the door
          a proper node of sound when you pass the right one
that has transmission, we were all doing the same art on cave walls
knocking our brains out
Did I hear right at Ajanta?
About how some were true and some false
No tonal contours of the architecture of cave
We heard her, another political ghost, in the car, older Vedic artist
rattling a mantra, on the other side
It does say that in the treatise the dead may rattle like echoing walls
a soundtrack of warning, especially those born in medias res
impression of sea pressures increasing on the eardrum
saddened by the El Niño effect
Talk about return, eternal, the winter solstice, rattles to attend a poem
Timpani in the symphony hall caverns
A tattled tale you conjure inside the cave when
Ukraine, Sudan, Gaza, Tiblisi are firing fireworks.

Trying to make it through—as the divination the cards said with a "Chariot"
How can you run a chariot underground?
Just standing outside the suffering not enough power in the drive shaft
between art eyes, with wheels on fire, eyes in motion
in Tarot, when upright, overcoming conflict, let's move forward
to enter her waterfalls, I drew that card, I would pull through
in the chariot I called "exertion"
adaptation . . . temperatures changing
or fast, takeover of the house after bust downtown
You can't see them. Think they are masked amassing on the stoop
maskless, and someone calls the Law you think?
What is law? Not allowed to make a right on red driving in a car, et cetera
May I memorize this painting one more time?
Will it be my rocket to when the well runs dry . . . ?
and find in hell or the underground siege
pitying the hostage a new eye, in gaze of fresh waterfalls
not ever see again law. You are dead.
Anarchy of the corpse
As energy pathways the paintings, migrations, marine animals
moving in, compete in joy for manifestation
Sustain life, Pat steers them, paint as blood, new veins
On the tongue, how you study the taste of uprising: in your own room
16 homeless on the floor sleeping, find them homes right now
Incendiary public servants, how you study the taste of blood, and previous
paint as nutrient
As science stumbles to do it better, a model
of disaster, I once trusted in all our work as
poet's blood life flow, a kind of telepathy-talisman
or crystal taste of water, inhumanity to harm the diseased
what we are willing to shed and pump up again
Talk about the time when astrophysicists did not do
the job for your generation and
so you grab on, an expert at the control, she
knew her service, locks all around her doors
look up, Antares! self-appointed

Then you could look up any way you wanted to then
Why not get off this into space
avoid a border in your rearview and embrace the invisible
And be glad it can be gotten, can "get ritual" as an implement
Buried in the ground will not attest to, aboveground data flow
have been studying the way social media is ripping us apart
hidden in crystal or secreted in an herb on a tree, hidden in
plain sight
or in the literal sky, all the mean things to warp a mind
you want to be a lover and an anarchist both? she continues,
in 2025? 2050? When you are outnumbered by the black & brown
All the theorists might doubt its theater if they lived long enough
People are complicated as was our mob scene, as throb & throng
Modesty is such a clue avoiding the abyss, critical
can we turn this around
is there political will? to stick with each other & anything?
We'll tell the story of *how to be better angels*
Bitterns, perhaps, how to be better bitterns
As if that is headliner that most worked-up word today "says it all"
is "unprecedented" as in a time how overused we all are in now
and victims, hammered, dented in servitude
precisely indented poetry indentured unzipped time, receding time
He-man America—long ago—id test—how it tastes in the mouth
as communication dissolves, devolves its clues
And still in racist hold, continually and as the
Text interjected all about freedom, funny word, mythological
This is *MY body*, and urgent
A memo of a heretical Cathar, her last memo . . .
spreading the dualist heresy
in language due in the first half of the 13th century
was the records of the Inquisition
women of beauty or ministers calls *perfectae* (contemplations!) or
    credientes (backbones!)
these were promised economic support and shift for the perfect idea of
"do what I want to"

Leave the beauties of studying Cathay and I will tell you, son
how finding converts to poetry, out of his fascist days, these days
Might be hard, China in ascension
my Mao is just a baby's toy, poet heralding romantically insane, swimming
    against the tide
And when the secret police also come to bust the poetry reading
Later, he held tightly on to, the occasion of it, to be poet and she said
"You'll be laughing but I always warned you it would start in radio
and spread to the next generations from public space"
Xi Jinping heeding the prophecy.
There was a lantern on before this nonsense started and the Chairman was
still on the money
There was an oil drum representing the beneficent sun and
       the Chairman was on solar time
But a beautiful way to behave if you love art, telekinesis, power
Sleeping in the charnel ground, and mimicking the sun with an old tin can
After Rangda some miles away sings and dances her bone-revenge soliloquy
    at crack o' dawn
There was no place to sit to hold, so crowded with rabble
You had to keep moving through the park
or through massacre in the hallways, trampled upon your costumes
Enough threnody & blood
no shelter in a hospital
Talked about poetry again, the deities out of their little shrines tonight
And what could a pilgrim be doing bathing in the spring of his freedom
His All Hallows' Eve city with friends, reveling he spent the night "in the can"
with his G-string costume on
Everyone wants one, little torture pilgrim, a parade, a mask, an occasion,
a rebellion
It's relative but from Ajanta, the resolute monk continued visiting your
    portal
Communing with the dead will be essential
After this colossal genocide
So we may know what the living really think of god, country, kingdoms
Muscovite pilgrims and all the rest

so we may know

mobsters wrapped up in the crime master's dream

Mustaches & loaves of bread

so we may know

Weak stew, hum of insects

"Tenting tonight" you will welcome the ladle

Down from the sky

A mouthful of speculation, dipper, drops down

to gather up earth's elixir while it lasts

and in the vision of something like Guadeloupe and she was a stand-in
     of all the

covert virgins

Also the pagan tantric deities of infinite power

who blow the systems to smithereens, they were stand-ins for all of us
     impostors

Who would burst out of molds & casts of plaster & bronze

To sit back under scrutiny again—What I wouldn't do! and be your
     favorite nun

Nuns were eschatologically sexy, entwined with the precepts of mind
     as it struggles

To wind up a world so you can live in it to wind up the doll in you as
     you become

an empty illusion

Then "it," our efficacy, needs to get to the next level, what will boost
     this consciousness

As we build our temple to the stars

All the obsolete who never die?

get us out of serotonin hell and the next level?

would be looking because they say the dead know

secrets, and "study harder"

Because they are struggling and need you

They half die, wanting to get closer up

When you are struck suddenly you don't know how to get out

and be old in secrets

And more of us disappear into the void, set up telepathy memorials

Suffice a climate for all exposure and take your power to the children
these legends of defiance I'll remind again a fury of fineries
not those who only know how to rule, but children who never learned
It was the women leaders of countries and countries that best
survived the catastrophe
even if it were axiomatic that
politics is the refuge of losers
But talk about what is it you learned about truth & beauty
and even if stale now, palpable
Don't be vague or in the vulgate we'll go there with them
Tear up things like "cares about"
Well I am about to study the life cycle again
I studied dominant men in the jubilant years
Was that a waste? trying to conquer them
And scares up a longer conversion
Dimming toward odd human and the queers I always knew inside myself
A poem-legend that tells you "tear off your epaulettes"
and tells Stalin's troikas where to get off
Is not so sympathetic when the nation goes awry
And flayed by systemic denial, let this leader go
"WE WERE ALWAYS QUEER" was the anthem.
Butting into other histories, candles lit
incense & mantra
in Nepal, Maruta said the migratory roads are ancestors now
My friend in Berlin says we are all migrants now
My friend in Sinai says she prefers the sea
And in Paris they go all official when challenged by trinity
(*liberté, égalité*) and money
My Turkish friend in Granada, Spain, repeats the restless ease of living
easy in poetic fraternity, but is it false?
and we are all participants
but where are poets studying now
study up or down? up? the new Babylon
the new earthquakes
Iceland relatively quiet

London we have not had the same welcome under Brexit
And my friend in Argentina: not all porteños condemn the change to: "a
    much better standard"
But we are all weary now
in living a partner's estate to keep them on
image of rising sun and image of setting and typifying a convenient form
declining immerses itself in the muddy sea for the new beginning
It will be tribal in twilight, an event horizon
inclination of the sun toward its setting, and low down
it is tableau, a marker for the next age installment
would be looking
up against tricky tides, a mimicking?
need an avatar my own body
heels as marks petroglyphs are useful
affinity, elbows the heft
In San Francisco, my friend says
old wells so down the rock we know well
but keep walking the incline, and the fire's omens
hell on earth
We both remembered the Song of Solomon
and John Coltrane's church
In the ancient conversation we remembered a New York School Second
    Generation
person, a memorial reader, asks about nexus, about love, okay to get it
    and I miss
the long walk by the East River before we fell before we left one another
stranded
and wrote about it, longing for Robert Desnos.
That is written toward a fresh volume, *Exiles in the Dark*
my newest declaration that the latest war started a long time ago
patriots in word of matter & darkness
surviving and bombed the duration
I am reading the authors of Kiev, women mostly
Dare a woe their clarity of icy times
I dance with Deren and wish to dress like Clarice

forms are not their present obsession
but migrants barely seen asleep on the pavement
near the Abolition encampment
on the ballot was the vote to keep the homeless away from your library
your neighborhood school, worried about "after hours" for the children
and you fought that space for them in time in language,
                survival of the brilliant scholars and the libraries
and in and out of wisdom with them, they mattered
they are life matter, I love the women most!
They are beautiful dust in all the galaxy
you will be wiser for the street, happy women! and men-women and
    children-women
the entrance is for you, wombs of texts
the street will have been your Nile, my trans friends
I am always missing your Berlin
the street will have captured your heart
and your head bashed by wanton cop, will be a badge you wear,
o badger? Identity you fight for, born in of
Telepathy means you are here on the wire
You will be wiser with what stands beyond
he, they—I will have captured your heart
telepathy is so amorous, as in Testo Junkie
Taking an inspiration means inhaling
the love-ark-heresies of St. Catherine of Siena
on her broken head
wait until she calms down
Wait and she will bridge all sacrifices of art
the socialist poet priest says indeed, and devotion
where there is no such thing as freedom in Capital
Waits to call over shoulder
Waits, while Turandot shakes a leg
The night the spirit in all the land
and wits are up again tonight flashing
Herminuisances of devotion, the priest says
and telepathy's the same music you play here: have to

work with vibrations of a lover in antithesis in laughter
Springlike rain then a dream then another
ritual, dining on squash blossoms
Then ravens flower over like a shadow-cloud
And go off in another tangent about Nicaragua
What could happen more what we didn't do enough of
Thinking about the Thessalonians
A state of mind
in a little hut on the palatial grounds
As we watch CNN rigged to jump up and fall and the planes
        flying overhead in Aviano
And on the other channels they were talking more tête-à-tête
not showing pictures of heavy battle
Do you remember where you are in each war?
How your heart feels
I got to Vietnam late and
walked past the corpse of a sacred warrior
was stilled by him, Ho engaged in flashback
when people are starving and murdered
What visualizations of the wounded you do now
And then in this short lifetime life got shorter from war
Because we needed memory devices
and couldn't afford them, and the young wounded
to be slaughtered earlier because we had run out of humanity to take care of them
you talked to the soldiers who came to meditate
Between the poets and their speaking
Between the poets absent in their writing
many had died
And the telepathy was going on . . . across all the galaxies, between
the devices and the echoes of the devices
After each death one heard a poem of the fallen
And when they passed there was a wave, wash, a clean sting of pain
Acts of intellection or it was some magic pause? is that the word?
Or it was illusion, as he said, and we all agreed, sexy wares in the rocks holding
up a very large bureau of time

what they are studying, the deceptions of rulers, continuing records of
    impasse
open all the drawers, the library is your new brain
I tell you I heard first the song of woe as it scribed in a book in a
prophetic voice which said there is no pause in samsara
And one of my teachers has said
It is all recorded, all the mirror images, like an inventory photo
you have seen what you have seen and it is loaded into you
who are a composite of forces enforced by what you are looking at
did you see me stoned by little rocks in Cairo? small boy urchins
did you see me hounded on the subway, beaten up on Avenue C
And messed up three times
Not one to whom a start of war is not natural
but a vocalization you can join in on as you fall
just studying? O clean again!
the boy who was clearly inspired contacted me.
"Ibu Anne" because I lead the groups to Tirta Gangga
and misplaced the ashes of the poet claiming India
Intellectus adeptus for the death cults
and I, teacher, was
kind of like the actor who took her little cart around villages
where we followed to see the shadow puppets
of Wayang Kulit when we wanted the way into psychic reflection
Where is she now? my muse
She was Italian, an actor, a scholar, Seraphina
I come back to her obsessively in perennial transit
Made with the holy skin of an animal, the puppets speak
in the disembodied voice of myths
that keep the whole psyche going below fear
Puppet animals skinned for this ritual way back, no worry
back then, no fear
In Java I studied my own biomes, and fear retreated
        at the full moon eclipse
And the deities were back in their boxes
and it was quiet

and this mood helped evolve our pleasure
Seraphina was rehearsing her lines behind the screen
we all called her home having witnessed
commedia dell'arte from a land far away, our great telepathy
her mind follows as trances a poet enacts
I loved her because she had been with me
during lifetimes, during the homecoming, during the cremations
during the conflagrations with all the worlds of art & memory
stronger, and their miraculous song
The rudiment ruins of sounds from instruments of iron
And lay my body down in the (neutral) charnel ground
curing the ceremony like we were in a crime scene and asked to testify
Heartbeat to the phrasing of this incremental forensic sound
All the demons of hell? Out to catch
To tempt, to shriek, to bang on iron
To turn again as if in fitful leap
When the wind left us and we trudged home tired
but joyous to our little compounds
for we had seen the world open wide, ironic and wild
Why and how and when and where we held not veiled destruction but our
implements were wool & metal to weave and shape again—and we
made beautiful soft sounds at dawn to
make the world again and our mind to snake and dance again
singing syncopated with the pace of the hooves treading, threading
my child asleep astride a donkey through the sleeping villages.

To Take the Measure
(Barometer)

- Matins (during the night, at about 2 a.m.) Watching, hoping for a plan, sometimes called Vigil and composed of two or three *nocturni* we shaped in the night. Nightwatch. Hoping for what came? Laura our cartographer was there one of the nights with us saying she would pray for lucid dreaming. We were camped outside the tight cloister, what luminosity inside? Coming off the desert. At dawn, a moment, rooftop in the city I could finally see my own hands in the dream.

- Lauds (at dawn, about 5 a.m., but earlier in summer, later in winter) Still up for the light. moon set. And we hoped for a message. To stay blessed and continued journey through Mexico, to our retreat of poets. Jacqueline with her apprehension, her Russian custom of dressing in shawls, a fartuk, wearing amber medallions of iconic Madonna. With lauds you count blessings, become speaking icons of supplication. *requiem aeternam dona eis, domine, et lux perpetua luceat eis, requiescant in pace.*

- Prime (first Hour = approximately 6 a.m.) A term that brings anything you want to the door. The animal, the jagged glass, a Buddhist monk, in the countryside outside Bologna with Gianni.

- Terce (third Hour = approximately 9 a.m.) City terseness, the cults' hour getting beyond the dawn work. "We are three, we sing three, we are three of the Trinity."

- Sext (sixth Hour = approximately 12 noon) A place for the living. Child born high noon and long. The waiting room at the airport, a stall, a pause, a baby born in such a transitory abode. A sanctuary for waiting flights in the night.

- None (ninth Hour = approximately 3 p.m.) Someone suggested "bury the dead."

- Vespers ("at the lighting of the lamps," about 6 p.m.) Outside, the protest, the park, voices, arrests, collapsing the tents, the violence. Extinguish the lamps. They say vespers take us through creation & sin, our traumatic expulsion from the garden.

- Compline (before retiring, about 7 p.m.) Trigger news, the night moves to the whole crisis as the world comes in. You try to let go. Never let go the End of the Day. Compline: you are the midst of it the mist in all. Another 100 murdered. Nakba. A giant canon of prayer from the Saint of Crete. We are called to a Name, leave us not, be sober be vigilant, o name of Lamb, whatever you are. Adversaries are everywhere in the struggle. Prowl, roar, devour, persist. Complicated, complicit. Small compline though all time: "ages of ages." Remember hostages. Liberate against suffering, don't toy with sorrow.

You are across a border when the returns come in, O never enough against atrocity . . .

May the fox who haunts the ruined mounds glide his tail . . .

May your clay bricks be returned to the abyss . . .

Illusion's Game

thinking patterns their

only ownership of   one and only

their only self. of that "this"

regard. et cetera
   it gripes for only
grasps
   dis
regard
        thinking

state
of
being a "doha"
            and fulfills the piling on of
forces, *kleshas*, studying existence

—*but are you experienced?*
question for a lifetime
            in transcendental vandalism.
and
        beliefs (compassion)
still theistic go for a

pledge
   to
warfare on the
battle
field

     do not look this way but please step aside
the sound or the sense?
   the hag says to Naropa who ran a school centuries back

 we went too far
we turn around, friend
 the sense or the sound?

 and cranberry rubies
 are set in pomegranate form
on the royal floor of
the great Stupa of Dharmakaya
 shine up at you, pebbles of enlightenment
 and glisten

and LED lights highlight kinetic sculpture of yab-yum
passion, red and
dark blue intellect fucking
  overhead
as agile feet stomp on eternalism
 & cynicism

 you try
to use
across all odds
your own assemblage
of divination, poetry's mother

you come out of a body's prison
studying spare parts
that's all we are? a series of folds?
ego nurses its ground
sharpens blade and things wake up as if
   existence studies itself

full-blown
  is over
and didn't just dawn on you

these rituals in the hallowed halls

    they'll hunt you down.

O tantric hunter,

I have drawn the arrow
    and make the target a kind of ecstatic pain
I'll catch onto, aim into, magnetize, destroy

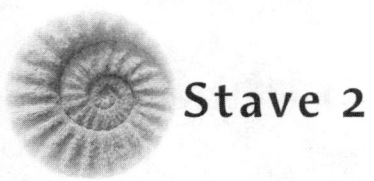 **Stave 2**

Slapped into night. / Dims into night. / A vessel. / Hidden. /
And another country and Nazis and turn-of-century martyrdom. /
Symmetries are likely in an audience too. / "Mirror me out," the child
says, tired of FaceTime / "I wish we all lived in the same city." / How
the indigenous experience viewed crystalized "Europe" / intricacies
of ablutions, ablations / nocturnes / the prophecies always had to do
with empire / So easy to rise and fall. / What was the music of that
sound? / Columns or bunkers of sound, for the cistern soldier citizen
/ the recordings for Radio Free Europe / waiting, and the dilemma for
Lieutenant Waldemann / out of the trenches to seek a dirge song, dead
shell shock daydreams for the savage mind. / Umbria: the troop of us
/ in a cabal, the priest guides us to the relics. / What is the mediation
after 9/11 but a fiery heart, world changed forever? / My student,
CIA, studying Arabic to translate an intercepted message. / To know a
system, listen to the music instead. Holy gimbri, oud, rababa, qanun.

"downstream without our knowing
  him: for if, he reasons,
  he can be overlooked, then to know
  him would be to eat him"

Nocturne: Cistern-like Symmetries

for J. M. W.

> *then there exists a magnetic stellar blackness*
> *a carnivorous oasis of blackness where*
> *the suns derive their power from obscurity*
> —Will Alexander

night here
one arrow for
floats
mode, this one is demon
seduction
navy-blue-dark officer still in
tantrums, purrs of collusion's
human? you have to wonder how
is node of escape
he wonders too, all the
making quantum physics
but you are
creating
and no one decides
bots of regression, the
itself, ghostlier ode in which
and you want to write poetry
create ode to a priceless
with glowing state
we'll get
and you're
leaving the universe
maybe this is
maybe
touch
maybe this
cut that

trobadour demons
each note
through traveling jongleur
impermanence this one
seduction of a
charge but on wane, rehearses
disillusion side of being
brain stem in off mode violent
for the reincarnated, enlisted
men do, men mostly
enough noise
assassin in charge
think tanks
without cunning
moon turns back on
you used to be loved
welcome eclipse,
red pearl orb up there
اللؤلؤة الحمراء أو هناك
alluwluat alhamra' 'aw hunak
building lights romantic music
the blue on the pearl
back in favorite Paleolithic
to its devices
canny darkness
innocence
my fear

and an epic told of progress
how creation
a language comes up
hurtling stones and
now they spurn you, powers,
about another dead rock star
monster of
what kind
world is secretly kind,
to the museum
always an immortal wishing
keeps you in focus
intrudes, reeks
counts time
my lover
lights a candle
cradle your aching
shoots barbs of projectiles,
why do they
we're here to make
lies turn cities to
words need to
spill whole magnitude in
hard to be in love but
as you escape
we still observe
your tattered wings
no identity to
as impostures for the
deeper magnitudes,
touch my heart and
touch the
sans eyes sans ears sans
touch belly's
urge let me rise and turn
the ten inhalations

you cross your heart
thought, maybe
in the bellies of nymphs
would be nocturnal
of grisly virgin sacrifice
birdsong, wind was an ally
what did she say yesterday
star in the room?
the mill
of win? for the music
but won't return
of sacrifices
for more attention
when a cruel tune
of nostalgia
and footsteps
my lover, a weathered rock face
for your handsome face
open your radical head
more assuaged, secrets
gear up, load up,
lie to us about creations
mating a new world!
dust, and detritus falls
be retracted from the snake demons
night's regressive tremors
love the words of love
the falling city, cry night owl
serpent deities who "dream as one"
tucked under a fallen city
hold this time, plummeting
fire, keeps edge on
stasis preferable?
where I have loss Promethean
vacant wound
nose sans everything

in the
it sounds
don't ever second-guess
a reckoning of shreds
and shots ring out
skeletons sway,
slinks in longhouses
another day
some musical victory
an inch on the
hey we're
hey, *au secours*
counting hours
crisis time we're
dream all hours in
drums minutes in systemic
come torque toward us,
all about a radiant
blue waves of
a clear melody floating
arpeggios,
sufficient
but you've got to get off
and *see* visions from atop
the retreat
mount of
concentration of
highest in three
and scientists agree
was on the surface of
analyze air
marooned in
flying wide above
my Masters and
Mistress Nod and
Molecular Madams will

sweet reward peaked in poetry
up this nocturne of loss
the luminous thousand things
witnessed after-hours
like this: bang bang
guess, but listen in Liszt,
and half notes.
in the old country concert hall
or electorate gets boozy
jog of ritual, gets ready
the (meat) wheel muttering
in the wings, a metered phrase
counting coup
shouting *CRISE CRISE!*
au secours! the slaughter
nightmare, turn down details
au secours! screaming you hear?
reversal scenario
cistern-like symmetries
then splayed
nexus or exit scenarios
retaliation, counterpoint
the staves on left hand above
break chords
in melancholia
the planet out of death trap
sky's dominance
ages of the ice
an ICE raid we witnessed
carbon dioxide
& you'll see a million years
a study of stomata
fossilized leaves
their pockets
Antarctic ice
become synthesized missiles

"see the little people"
another succubus liberated
clues me in misunderstanding
go now, nightmare, so petty and
speak in obscure night
reticence for revenge,
I won't shut up but
be stilled, "metabolism
memorize your
for a
night's dominance
and her
with hyper-activated
and you will see into the fear within
not handing you a drug
and cry your
but don't waste time while
"Hey! way to go!" growing
anything you want in
be a thousand words for
and steal her
rollick a long day in
decision in the wicket in
ayahuasca is ancient
before it was
or human's guilty woe or
and could read
read hours, put the
and listen to the earth
and chatter of
to vomit the
bury in, retreat, barrel down
an echo, nothing
in this time of
to circle and
but you are

their religious agendas
with serene pleasure
whisper in soft repose
people just squeak by
beyond binaries for pleasure
cosmic silence
suffocating as I douse
tongues" don't denigrate
fury knows no restraint
beg it shuts me down
of centuries
new name,
poetry tournament,
of the prisoner Anne,
battle for Archive
sense protectors
this costly lens
in spoon but drink this
heart out,
it stops a sec for another
back of skin, reptile woman
your alterity groove
Mistress Chance woos her
footstool, her hum
another new century
the ballot in the body
immortality clung to a vine
plant or man,
was just an ear listening
flowers, read leaves
cup to your mouth
moan and heave
pixels lock you in
universe
another mountain to ring around
here to win

and you are
what new planet's moon
won't you
reconstitute in
ever more duty in
lap-in-motion paralysis
I didn't order
put down your defense
re:
cyborg warriors come
let the rider
measure
temperature,
what do I pay
what is a
have your
light escape path then
sleep tantra,
visualizing a
seed syllable
good to come
some wilderness
can't fake
where is our
Mt. Meru here
center of the universe,
nocturne paired
come on the heels of
or Chopin, imitations of
a far-off sound, a
peak of a
future that first summer
no one
female choir singing between
won't ever be
tranquil

peregrination you know best
dances with elves
mastodon Armageddon
shatter hard getting it on
you being on how new moons
descend
never sleep
new plasma
re: post consciousness
not the game today
that up, cynic,
mechanism reboot smile
fuel
out to test the water
dip a foot in muddle
silvery moonlight
night tax for sound?
day tax for havoc, the political
torch nearby
enter bardo's divine yoga club
keep breathing,
shimmery "AH"
of surprise
down the tunnel
sorrow in Cecil's lament
it anymore
rose continent
pyramid to climb
exhausting all meditation?
horn with spring
jazz, a wartime serenade
twittering birds
betterment, a moment
solstice, like jazz peaks
a wet dream
saved

try it? not
no one but you
and go batten down
get safe model,
with a safety
of genderless
distinctly perfumed line drive,
won't care but
can you see into
find Debussy's lost soldiers
in "Trois Scenes"
with its mysterious
who pass us
wait in line, suckers! gin
because the night
because the night more
because the night
because
we stopped
you think a
because it's night?
a stunt, the rock concert
sometimes misjudged
hellish footsteps
assault, of what is a
old stars were lost to poets
reckoning
move away we want
the morning
and ready if we must
مات شاعر وحيدا لأن ليله؟
mat shaeir wahidan li'ana laylhi?

notes of tranquility
enough in this pastourelle
saboteurish,
saved, time's sisters
our hatchless imaginary
our premiums,
lock the vessels
persons, critical
gussied up for a kill?
blast and destroy
this nighttime? lost three seconds?
like a manuscript
"au Crepuscule"
songs of Sirens
passed by, laughing:
lit up with a new motive
the treaty broke
raids more bombing
a poet died lonely
the night
remembering the tune
nocturne is easy?
it's a magnum work
job, a soldier's lament
with fluttery hands
like traipse of a giant
the price of
but left instead trace of sound
tried to, could soften?
to know all the answers
after battle and be armed
the father cries out

"(with victory) to disappear?"

Let go the world around us old as water   as crystal mirror
primordial in the hand of the roving eye   toward future
trees memory   in the belief in the alterity   in a plea   a gesture
ascending toward the first and last cause   at the edge of precipice

Nocturne: Martyrdom

"You should study the green mountains, using numerous worlds as your standards. You should clearly examine the green mountains' walking and your own walking. You should also examine walking backward and backward walking and investigate the fact that walking forward and backward has never stopped since the very moment before form arose, since the time of the King of the Empty Eon."

—*Master Dōgen*

"Is it really big enough?" Niels Bohr asked J. Robert Oppenheimer in December 1943, the day he arrived at Los Alamos, where the Americans were secretly inventing the new bomb. Oppenheimer understood him immediately: Would it be big enough to make war impossible?

did a movie not really stop the next war?
never will. apparently not. genocided

        sacrifice's verbal accommodation
as zones demand a free trade of bodies
summon insulated axon hillock

arrive   arrive. have been studying movies
              and more arrived

sacrificed in a worldly way
put an idol or god on the dash
little red Mao or crucifix
of Santa Niños
Che in a dream
      a new hero—terror?
          have been studying Dōgen

how raw? I . . . kept traveling
Che . . . a dream

Africa, raw of immigration,
back back

grammar modules in body after sinewy body
hike over borders
or seeing oneself a ritual offering to zones of dominance
where "gradualism" & "developmentalism" go together

mano a mano

many women understand this, this generation
and flee back to the cinematic to
understand the "auteur" syndrome, poet be wise
take control of the scenario, the mise-en-scène,

is she already human? she transferred a body
toward progress, we could not be these gendered humans
           quite the same anymore

we park the car to study some Etruscan tablets
mores of the interesting dead ones,
     the Pyrgi, a treaty

(Ernesto my companion is cautious   hesitant)

sea power was waning
    Phoenician and Etruscan language
quibble over words for "king"—
      lauxum or *zilac*
a magistrate?
        commemoration of the death of Adonis
important rite . . . death of a handsome one

and another tablet on Astarte:
may the years of the statue of the deity be as numerous as stars

"it was at Assisi my conversion"

nervous as stars

mind twisted chant upon plainsong, starward

first communion

"it was in Angola my conversion"

turned the mind
you might visit starry Gubbio

and it sounds "nubile" speech awaiting human context
fortuitous alternations human larynx all synaptic voices calling yes
invoke the no voice and all or none of it calling no not yet
women line the road for hire

it sounds human desire
in site of sex, to converse

an expectation
gaudy apparatus and stunning
a night you nudge gently to hide
don't send me back to the hospital
or if you must, send me off to bed and may we sing through suffering
through martyrdom, these times a cause be of that woman doom
and no sway

if they won't sing . . . and me a saint and Ernesto a priest

                                bend for the succulent grape
                          eye level of the grass down from the trees
                     some vestigial belief system. ethos of survival

                                              euros of survival

get these cuffs off! (Ernesto, *the commie priest*)

but then again you might be stuck in the mind that thinks it needs
    containment
sacrifice   slogans   nervous brain relic of St. Catherine

                   or scar of red in the Blombos Cave,
splash of ochre on a firelit wall

77,000 years ago children tended flocks

and anticipated *la Revolución*

a choice for the jihadist woman
detonate
or not?
the
serpent
at
her waist
or no

and Virgin St. Arilda of Gloucestershire goes down martyred for chastity

        no free lunch?
we argued. he was certain red he was certain cerulean blue
the angels mocked the sure belief system you cry between bouts of secular &
    sacred . . .
            I paid

the ruling cartel laughed Uccello
excursions in the back wheat country, land grabs Uccello! Uccello!
physics came first of gravity of pigment soaring gold nimbus
stage blood tears fell as diamonds my eyes could see
hallowed glories, rays pierce stigmata
wax going down in the sacristy
hold out the palms
chemistry followed and we know the blend & brevity of holy seasons
it grows it grows
ample for martyrdom
geology or biology by the 19th century

        scribes in sync with the rules, regulation pleasure's a wary sister

and servitude & evolution waver between tears, diamonds, blood

supremacy ruminating heroic human deeds

    of animals, too and
their acts of kindness & generosity not like ours
never mistake the smile of the diamondback snake
    her hum

yet trembling sacrificial animals—such as this lynx—with magic powers

Ernesto & Uccello, the horses

Eugubine valley is the majesty of Umbria

        its Zona Rosa, of communist tinge, color endemic to ethos of
  village
famous for rituals of craziness & redemption

                you have to keep council

tiffs over Vatican and its Spanish martyrs could ensue

inside press up against an act sweetly politic

you have to seem to be as resilient
seem sexy on the outside so as not to reveal your secret seemly
  weaponry
I just say that with bravado I am really outside the night
savannah in her hair seen from headlights
her back presses on grass, we whiz past
  Surrealism I go crazy in all her wild tresses

plug in
this is test of one's allegiance to rapprochement between East & West
& Old Europe
        and how we incorporate a modern view of ourselves
Asia in wings? All blown to bits, the fickle wind

what in modern biology has roots grown on Buddhist philosophy?

                or on tongues & arms of Shiva?

back to the grass's different angle now, Islam's lens
    pressure of desire is hypnotics
haunts illusionists no image no image
    sell our bodies to the highest bidder but cover your eyes first my girl
my girl my gruel

the jobs with "stationary machinery pending" is her power
            yet she rules me her martyrdom
                                        messages . . . there's a boat
in her face lusted for

what has desire to do with the subject of martyr?

                everyone has a price for suicide

decorative hand patterns, stick people & hunting parties
your face

    (our freedom cell resisted the hunt, boycotted it, but devours the rabbit)

                         she wondered her recombinant
power
     for
the
     hunt
                         virgins wait in heaven

martyrdom as performance

    Purify your heart and clear it from all earthly matters. The time of fun &
waste is gone. The time of judgment has arrived. O God you who open all
doors, open all doors to me.

martur = to witness, to attest
     wonder influence ripples in the night, intentionality,
neurotransmitter release
          or sucks off nipples, mutters revenge

I can't tell my brain tissue from yours it's so ideologically framed

               wonder what is current below
you all get below
and wonder the many glia that surround your neurons

          would she be big enough to make war impossible?
critical current ferrets you out
  as you get with that flow
                    Andromeda a galaxy far away
so far a relief I don't have to worry about it waves off

what is the influence of Africa on our potentialities and
               would merit end of war in all quarters?
my brave accomplices, weigh in
what strikes is odd juxtaposition to ask this question now. white and supreme

what is the wrench to not roast me here now
in front of all my people

shard glaze shard red dirt tile roof all translate as a safe house

                              (*the prophet was always optimistic*)

as in the movie *The Edge* a young Anne plays the wife of
the terrorist
        and he has to hide (in the safe house & not-so-safe house)

someone sniffed the air (was cool it was autumn just so you know)

                        could this be doubted in a ghost world

and Anne (as actor) said:

We walked along the beach it was the beach at Deal. My husband, who in real life
    was my
        friend Tom
    He was going to assassinate the president
  I can't remember, did it work out?
And one heard voices then saying "on" or "turn left now" your face to him endures

he has a toy gun in this act of choice & purpose
  under the shadow of the mega bomb

stone floor . . . when my struggle

autumnal sweep . . . when my struggle when my struggle

dialogue was something like this:

— how long will you away and acting so odd and all? and how long
from me away
little homunculus in the brain
(*pause*)

— it's a secret and locked up in hatred of empire, that terrible white
house, et cetera.

[takes place in D.C., there were some rooftops & long shots of avenues]

— so I can't speak of it? the secret package & pact you shelter and keep
and haul around?

the beach was deserted, a shelter likely for this man or boy, the other people
are at table fall swirling round us, climate of Vietnam,
anger about secret bombings in Cambodia smart beings being imploded in
anger against
empiricism, that terrible house, et cetera.

what chilly forest is this? or psyops

I implore you, one said, can't take it anymore

terrible terrible house

a monk on fire he wanted us to know this all of him to see
and later in Burma, the spirit of him passed to Burma
& Tibet . . . it passed the spirit of immortal to that place . . .

————————

bow down
task where danger
lies within zealotry

within officers, within
mukhabarat borders
homegrown

————————

and if you want to see or be seen as guest worker burn up right now
    not let nervousness
show if you want to ride not quite your gentleness show tough as you
    might be
in an American safehouse shelter you'd be inside that thought of shell
    shock burn shock though blind own
pasts and burning
    (she survived, his *grand-mère*, the recent bombing in London . . .)

and if you want to protest of course you are one who has a fairly stable
    mind, a parallax view
please do so and burn, burn one life the shock of its choosing this over
    a lifespan of paranoia

or crucible in which you are forged is never enough for auto-da-fé
      we made love the director didn't take our clothes off
But the disaffected cold ones that were our "enfranchised" leaders
      became a kind of frigid
stability

but it's one thing to die solo for a cause not taking innocents as you go
    down, down
      another down trend owned

a freeze on times

true memory

false memory, are you trending?

true

false as the director of my hope & fears of actor-being

and your hero is always locked down (emotion) but running she hiding (motion) in performance

and you say that with highlights resisting, of highlight modes she resisting, times, or anger of those times: he, the assassin playtime villain

drive single road very fast the car from the Italian castle

trialation   triangulation

. . . and Óscar Romero the peoples' saint of El Salvador assassinated saying mass in the hospital

chapel of the Carmelite sisters

———————

impassioned mullahs
can't pry open
the Arab door, nothing
came. No information
came but the video
of grim execution

———————

and feel it again now we're on the wavelength my ancestors: sanctuary

      insist sanctuary
because
    you / I, start to explode
in expediency to "take" "someone" "out"

the times, we say admirably, the times, the times, and "back" "then" or
"foolish" "back" "then" repeating and knowing "then"

   Bobby Seale insists

take these off
cuffs & gag

and all the others
someone is watching us
took the flash of synergy
     colors were black and white, edge of industrial cities, black and
  white
flash of synergy
flannel, black and white and you go and stand up for someone
even if it means you are shunned in the whole mercenary house

     covet my speech then

al-Hallaj

  the one enraptured says

tie me up, gag me

we were closer to surveillance and to knowledge of our "lot"
  and under   a strobe   a flash
  adjacent to a woodshed   weapon   pile of leaves
someone is watching us who abandoned her post by the lake
  and took the road
through the desert remember?
 it was our first movie abiding motion

     women-many-aliases said, it was ours, our "time"

———————————

Benedicta's feast day May 10

Sant'Alphius's tongue ripped untimely from mouth
Cyrinus boiled alive
Philadelphus burns

(did Abbie Hoffman keep a gun? you'd asked at
the strategy meeting)
   you mean, would he give me one?

(movie dialogue is adequate here an awkward reality flared up on their
   relation to one
another
 pause, silence
  how far you would go as a pacifist)

     closer to a place that would be exploded

— we have a cage for you, just like a canary, or will you sing?

       ◆ this one weighs no more than 162½ pounds
       ◆ there must be thousands of signs from the heavens up there

— we'll find the sign I'm sure

     — come on, I'll buy you a soda
     — Skyland Playground of The World

       ◆ Club Doré
       ◆ Floor Show, Olympic Café
       ◆ request answer
       ◆ close the folder sorry
       ◆ sorry can't find the real imposter
       ◆ can't help no martyr stories
       ◆ but the threat all around
       ◆ and the last word *Allah*
       ◆ a holy word

and you knew the woman who survived the town house explosion, exited
in one piece

hid many years (some said Russia or Cuba) and surfaced
    and went to jail many more years for her part in a fatal robbery and died
her mother wept in the kitchen and once put her head in an oven
could say a site surfaced in her bright clear mother blue eyes said careful, be
    very careful
she the mother survived with dear blue eyes the notorious lawyer her husband
    commented yes they are indeed "twinkling" be careful be very mindful

----

toxicity whose law is not helped by habeas

look there, accomplice
because you look there and you are added in
    (someone suffers) you are an accomplice
    you mull it over in the prison yard

under the cloak of amber, under the
    Russian she studies be careful all my accomplices

    man and a language go underground in amber
glasnost site of body ready to move

along a corridor glasnost

Molotov   glasnost

metabolism glasnost glasnost
    glasnost the Moorish landscape

glasnost glasnost
or plan

that includes glass

      woman of Ávila for one, did she wish a plan
can we see a matrix of plan in her wish

    in praying for martyrdom?
did she—
el sueño—survive?
she lived long and not lose faith

a drawing is useful *is*
a bullet *is*
thorns *is*
a bell *is*
alembic

not burned like some at the stake

is suspicion at wrist

and signs from higher power insist on service

I tell you I did hear voices, didn't I?

is cold luster that made everything for the moment look hard and ugly

is downside of occupation, what the devil are they doing here
        at the empty bombed-out shrine

woven of other things
        representing the five senses,
               the sixth being mind

    is softer tone to sky what in the name of heaven & earth and all the
    reasons of love
               are we doing here

        track the confidence men superweapon snake oil men

---

keep dying Fidel afloat
Ostpolitik or
sell tanks
to Egypt & Syria
bomber gap
missile gap
smoke & mirrors

---

mighty strong Satanic arc
    ambient light here in the territories
ever occupied where the movie stops
    upon a place where someone will die

a wall or lot as vacant as dead eyes a rooftop

the seer said tell her in her last lifetime with dead eyes she'd let her
    people down

so she'd come back to repair the crisis that allowed this people down

but Daw Aung San Suu Kyi never lets her people down, but
    occasionally
        or does some political
during protests the monk at her door her face in the doorway
hands in *anjali* to greet them house arrest 12 years but never never
    never
never lets her people down
then she does, but survival?

love righteousness ye judges of the earth

(and how all fades in the struggle of "never let")

take your place
"so that was the hook," she said
and "come back to repair"
and "never let them off their genocide"

mention abdication of power as with Socrates

that's one idea
the other was bright day walking around, more you saunter she tells
    the guy
maybe stop it   being so obvious   the park in Berlin
     where they gathered, many people, mention Turkish ones, a
    picnic
and later in the theater
    some would rise to protest, denounce the site, the tent, the event,
      imperial authority white
German poetry the poetry of American ones that occupy the park

amplified sound of occupation
putting their words on top of topos of picnic site
and often music & dancing negated here on top of topos

fill space
you own it
amplify it I said that already
how many decibels
before the gorgeous activist girl
pulls the plug
she holds up her fist
scarf around her fate

out in the space of a park
families and ladies in flowered scarves
dusk now little lights cookstoves

I think of them forever as Turkish they could imprint that way
coming a long way from Turkistan
flowers in the struggle

flowers on scarves

I saw them in Iran she said maybe they come of there

suddenly she seized it, young, too young, she on the microphone
    denouncing all over again
young the microphone I remember this, the stage, surprise

and the famous novelist next to me

Günter leaps up

denounces them Nazis Nazis! he shouts
(the imposter too?)

give us our stage and she gets carted off with a rose in her fist

carded insult
these not citizens under draconian law
not not ever citizens even by birth here
      on this spot
never let the people down

and what to think but how culpable the victors some are
                  Kreutzberg
         he who revealed later his own Nazi youth shouting Nazi Nazi
         and how what is hidden is prophecy in how it is acted first
         and then revealed later what's hidden what's revealed adds up
                  flush in an
                  angry Nazi voice

            vocals are shards

         his body leapt up, flush, in an angry voice, shards that could add up to
                  Nazi! Nazi!
well you can't have her dying a noble death that would make a martyr of her
shot by bullets exploded in a suicide blast too risky die martyr for her cause
            cause of avenging father cause of democracy
can't make a martyr of her now it's already happened it happens martyrs will
                  happen
      make up story make it unseemly not the death of a martyr hit by lever of
                  sunroof how
secular it sounds "lever" "sunroof" how unseemly not the cause for death of
                  a martyr "lever"
         "sunroof" could have happened anyway not in the middle of
         chaos as this suicide bomb & shrapnel & gunshot wounds
      how much more martyr is "gunshot wounds" is "suicide bombing" is
                  "democracy"
narrative call it master so "secular" so "patriarchal" no women at all around her
      they say now skull fracture when she was thrown by the force

of the suicide bomb and
hit her head on the "lever" of the "sunroof" of the car in which she was riding
not enough protection, blame the martyr
can't unmake a "martyr" now too late to unmake "martyr"
but for this she will be "martyr" certainly no matter "lever" no matter
"sunroof"
but matter "democracy"

"democracy" "loaded" "as" "well" "as" "being" "lauded"

with Negroponte with a loaded history

———————————————————

"I had no idea I had nourished a viper at my breast"

                    to be forcible as wit & measure he's no martyr
                                              to burn books
                                               blood is real

              and the others getting bashed, just a few youths down
                          the neighborhood that way you go

                       a Panther you nod to in the doorway
                             at the after-school program
                                        now swept away

I was in my past life, the table, swept
people drinking
passed them earlier, away
how could we love each other in a better world
and a tent set up for dreaming a little social construct

this was then
and then just (innocent) drinking

                    _____

                                                    O serious Trotskyites

where did the red-bearded talker friend go who gave such confidence
                                                            in his acts
or the other, where is he now?
                                    squat demonstrations and other acts of
        noble anarchy
last glance at the street demonstration
                        he'd found his instrument to be a video camera

where now?
                        Ancient Ikuvium:

they run through the streets widely, carrying the *ceri*, heavy wooden posts
topped with statues of saints

and run all the way up the slopes of Monte Ingino
and nearby a gorge with the best-preserved sequences of deep ocean limestone in
    the world

the Cretaceous-Tertiary boundary zone
which contains an unusual concentration of iridium, iridium
the maker of the asteroid or impact that led to the extinction of the dinosaurs

and on the Mexican border Blackwater wanted to build an 824-acre mercenary camp

                    _____

go to death

they all go to death.
where are they now?

in the Whitney, Henry Taylor's humanity

and you are in the last light Brad Will went out in before Oaxaca

    and you wanted to pick him up gather up pick him up pick them all up
        like children from
the grass and wash their wounded bodies

Slinky Blue of Umbria I sing to myself say don't sell your body, Slinky Blue
and Brad Will you still be slinky red anarchist, there now rest now? how
        many memorials
until we find your killers? mercurial times? fast times to oblivion justice
and all the saints of Italia asleep in their tombs
relics of blackened tongues . . .

but never rest the bottom of these the deeper in you have to dig the
        crematorium
and below the bedrock
silt and shadow . . . cryptic

[a curtain is not their metaphor]

when my investigative rage when my struggle . . . but never end

intaglios from the shaheed *world*

Civitella Ranieri Center, 2001–2024

Some Weave in the Poem
(of Nocturne: Martyrdom)

a free trade of bodies . . . Many Nigerian women, primarily from Edo State in the south of that country, have been lured to Italy (by various organized crime syndicates) to work as prostitutes. I saw many stunning and desperate women mostly on the outskirts of Gubbio, soliciting from the bushes. *Ernesto is cautious* . . . Ernesto Cardenal (January 20, 1925–2020), the Nicaraguan poet and Catholic priest who served as minister of culture for the Sandinista government from 1979 to 1987. He is author of the epic *Cántico Cósmico*. We were together on a residency in Umbria right after 9/11 and argued about the notion of "free lunch." [See my interview with him in *Outrider* (La Alameda Press, 2006).] *nervous brain relic I thought* . . . The small, desiccated head of St. Catherine resides in the Basilica of San Domenico in Siena. As it was being smuggled to Siena in a bag, it turned temporarily into hundreds of rose petals to escape notice. *or scar of red* . . . Blombos, a cave in a limestone cliff on the southern coast of South Africa where 75,000-year-old beads from *Nassarius* shells and 80,000-year-old bone tools were found. It is thought that the people associated with this site behaved in a cognitively modern way and had syntactical language. *as in the movie* . . . *The Edge* (1968) is a film by USA filmmaker Robert Kramer (1939–1999), founder and prime mover of the Newsreel project. I had a brief role in *The Edge* playing the wife of a terrorist who plotted to kill the president of the United States. *and Óscar Romero the peoples' saint* . . . Óscar Romero (1917–1980) was the archbishop of San Salvador who organized on behalf of the poor & disenfranchised of his country. He was assassinated while leading a mass by a right-wing group under the leadership of Major Roberto D'Aubuisson. Canonization has been initiated in the Roman Catholic Church. *Bobby Seale insists* . . . Bobby Seale (born 1936) was cofounder of the Black Panther Party for Self-Defense, founded in 1966. He underwent extensive FBI surveillance as part of the COINTELPRO program and was severed from the Chicago Eight trial (subsequent to arrests during the 1968 Democratic National Convention protests) for his periodic outbursts in the courtroom. He was bound and gagged by Judge Julius Hoffman and sentenced to four years in prison. I participated in protest events during the trial (with Allen Ginsberg, John Giorno & Michael Brownstein) and witnessed Seale's troubling plight "as a shackled slave," someone said in the courtroom. *and you knew the woman . . .* Kathy Boudin (1943–2022) was the daughter of the high-profile liberal lawyer Leonard Boudin and the poet Jean Boudin. She was a member of the Weather Underground and spent 22 years in Bedford Hills Correctional Facility (for her part in the robbery of a Brink's armored car), where she initiated important parenting education, adult literacy, AIDS, and women's health programs. I knew her briefly as a child—her mother was a close friend of my mother, Frances LeFevre Waldman. Kathy won an international PEN prize for her poetry in 1999. See the excellent documentary *The Weather Underground* (2002). *and the famous novelist next to me . . .* Nobel Prize–winning German novelist Günter Grass (1927–2015) was sitting next to me at a poetry festival in 1976 in Berlin when he jumped out of his seat to denounce young Turkish protestors. He revealed in 2006 that he was in the Waffen-SS in the early days of World War II. *well you can't have her dying a noble death . . .* Benazir Bhutto (1953–2007) was the first woman elected to head a Muslim state. She served as prime minister twice and was assassinated at a Pakistan People's Party rally in Rawalpindi on December 27, 2007, two weeks before a Pakistani general election in which she was running. The cause of death was first announced as shrapnel wounds to the head, then finally attributed by Scotland Yard to her head hitting a knob in the car she was traveling in after the impact of a bomb. Al-Qaeda was most likely behind her death. Her financial dealings were shady, and although her enemies called her the "most precious American asset," her mother reportedly made the "viper" comment quoted in the poem. It was the shadowy reportage around her death that triggered this meditation on the "master narrative" of martyrdom. *with Negroponte . . .* John Negroponte (born 1939), whose power & influence extended over the "dirty wars" and many violations of human rights carried out by the Honduran government, in which thousands of Hondurans were tortured and executed. Under his watch, military aid from the US to that country—

deemed necessary to build a bulwark against the revolutionary Sandinista forces "next door"—grew from $4 million to $77.4 million. He was an obstructive ambassador to the United Nations, succeeded Paul Bremer for one year as ambassador in Iraq, and was the first Director of National Intelligence, a cabinet-level position. *the last light Brad Will went out in* . . . Brad Will (1970–2006) was a spirited anarchist activist and Indymedia journalist who was murdered on October 27, 2006, by Mexican-government-backed paramilitary forces while filming a teachers' strike in Oaxaca. He filmed his own death, which can be seen on YouTube. Brad was a friend and a frequent attendee during the summer sessions of the Jack Kerouac School of Disembodied Poetics at Naropa University in the 1990s. His murderers walk free. New wars, what memory reconciled from old. Cretaceous to now. The war map dominates a section of the brain. James Baldwin said, "See the forest through the gaze of hanging bodies." Fight-or-flight. Fears & panic of the amygdala. The fakest century unsolved. Unresolved. *Shaheed* means "witness" in Quranic Arabic, but the term is also used for Muslims answering a commandment as "martyr."

Stave 3

Druid is knower of the oak tree. / Druid listens to the oak / an old societorcery. / Stop in a methodology of hiddenness, or stardom / 56 million years ago, genus *Quercus*. / 435 species, Canada to Andes, / Norway to Indonesia. / And we pretend the forest in our fallen city a sacred garden / pretended the incident we did to portion it all / as we went hunting / we say "the wood axe, the wood axe did it" / we had gone to the woods during the long plague we went often to "out back" / we hauled water / we lit fire / what we could avoid / we pretended we were really old / invisible / had lived many eons / we pretended boldness when we were scared / but it's real and we notice / rings of the wood, blood rings, marbles & habits / handmaidens of time / little child Luna Luz had her / chest cut open to save her heart / we were flying in fear / and we cheated it out, and chased out fear in the rings of time / pushed out our fear to help her live / one so young / and more of the civilizations were raging / in their war habits, this beautiful Luna Luz and her kin / and the rings were blood but lifelines / in the sorcerer's eye / she conquered, she lived. She walks. / She sings.

"ingest the name he carries through time to set down"

Sorcery: Times of the Chthonic

Preface

"moan" "inside" "wood"

   sors:
of casting magic lots a billboard rail station,
old drive-in, rustle up a roadside ritual

sortis:
. . . erotics
   be sure to tie shimmering   speaking of name
rainbow knots   & mirror
to weather
now this way. That   the poet
   up & down   has
your hand in cinematic rhythm.
sprocket lock.   body.   identity:
birds tethered to an A-frame shelter   pensar
cockfight brought from Persia through Greece?

   hurl ribboned thunderbolts,   against the interlocutor
spurs   locked in silence
moaning inside wood   exiled from the cambra

love laments a leg spread to chaos   a
   and sooty bird eyes crack open   burning
                                             cross

priestesses divine   convert the infidel?
pronouncements
      listen to the leaves

why do idiots fall in love?
sorcery remembers
shadow people. malcontents
sparagmos of mind,
the divination of dead animals
(are we even people yet?)

a long night eye slowly
moving, tent's ghost light
in rare opening
flicks of
        hazelwood
from the caravanserai camp
     splinters a
dousing
for honey. are we?
your screen goddesses
queens of bees?
golden honey
down to earth
important for gravity's
pull-down?

      friction tucking poetry
in bed
stars awake desire
chaos, dumb
speak only poetry?
ensorcelling pulchritude

breasts spew ashs
volcanoes morph
a magnetic charge
agents of axis shift
douse for blood, as

be
the
     lyre of another's
wooden   skull?

earth-hood,
mouth is
spiral
a cradle for fabrics
and civilization is
weather's
erosion
sedimentation
litho foliations
destruction fast-track
planet-lungs exhausted
consumed in flames
inextricably,
in curse of prime capital
what is syntheses for the
nursing mother
all need rescue,
now empires turn poisonous
this is the time of exorcism
up in smoke? In flood?
this is the time
of an owl's eye
seedpods at wrists
at ankles
falcons up sleeves, to make noise and flutter
this is the time
refract a mirror in brain
to shift axis
tree in wind, bends
a battered hell
roil, turn, spool the film and start again   seen
a cybernetic mist   on
sorcery's desire of matériel..   an oak tree scan
this is the time
the suck-up

last calorie
of fossil fuel
out of
tissues
you migrate
canal & ditches
you cross safe for
escape
an epic canticle
sung by future children
where to find
the witchity grubs
how to fill the water jugs   root
best place to lie   up and
down,
it wasn't over yet

this is the time
what road moves
circling?   from teeth
backward out of a mirror   a book
sex & eyes, time to
render rest of nature?
silent and obedient
render freedom?
what rules a world moaning
and grinds on top of
operatic maiden behind
a cloister
as Greenland loses
160 billion tons
of surface ice
23-foot rise in global sea levels
in a bed of words
have a museum
& homeless shelter?

at the same time
bends to gather
token of chance
start a new wheel
listen, my little ear
the rune: of the terrible politician who ruined the lives of
everyone will testify on the rigged skyline, face jail time
the slyer, never gets caught

1st hour (apt to dial)

Harry Smith's film #12
of Buddhism & Kabbalah

of
sorcery is a mantra
and the wood cross section

agaric mushrooms

mantra remembers

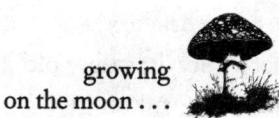

it of all "it," whose face on the
clock? how many
answers in rune

growing
on the moon . . .

where a hero &
heron ride by

cracks & pops syllables
a poem under my skin
transmigrate to
screech late or early?
primordial acceleration
in speed of retrieval

on a cerebrum

in the first watch:
scratches of recognition to say
"earth-matter"
are we late or early?
the dawn this talent
bandwidth
apt to dial, rotation
involving nascent Macouri
when it's all passed around
a round of singing
are we early or later?
the first watch

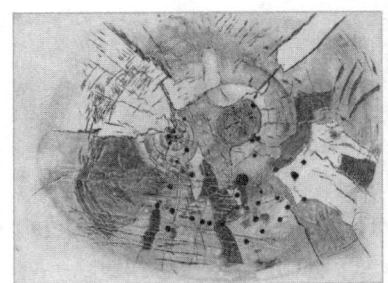

2nd hour (take to task)

late, danger

shed snakeskin
attest to bravery!
just safety, it, safely old
body's morphology
measure of form
catastrophe of words
propeller wings
spine's alliance
triggers linguistic
planetary shifts,
coils in the strophe
volcano's release
coils dark hole

a
snowflake
a single flake
        expands the

        cabalistic

Tree of Life

center of star, of rooster
meteor in space, coils   jutting on Ventadorn's
spores & slags   *joi-dolor* antithesis
cracks, dents   ignore the
inchoate lines   principle of *meʒura*
transmigrate, and coils   (moderation)
sapwood's lifeblood
acceleration of coils
to desire, to "task"
fractured coalition   Lombarda's
Anthropocene   many selves arise in Bernart's *cobla*
in the Garbo stratosphere   (*la dousa votʒ*)
reins of the humana
lighting a face   but she is a mirror-figure
take center   who becomes a speculum:
off human?
gilded age, a mixed bag   where is her *tornada*?

3rd hour (crosshatch/nazca lines)

breasts
eyes
mortise & tendon joints
every animal
invoked here
and photosynthesis
her seer-self
going after the winged
growls and explodes

makes gesture
crosshatch
concentric Indra's   a bird lands on   the zenith of
brain stem
pupils dilate to   a spiraling scroll
greater purpose
of how your
ocean cracked
how
brain coral
of first lover
died and cracked
a code of patterns
become limping
code to limbs
transform by energy
substance is alchemy
in the mix,
reverberations
why does she stare, like a crazy girl
life okay in the Holocene?
or isn't it time to leave?
This came from you,
Oneiropompus,
conductor of the dream
Jean Harlow voice raised
sarcastic wits send up her youth

4th hour (invasions)

kinesthesia's
sweet purpose
plumes of tears
smoke the stage
eyes bleed tender
inscription a test
register for her aria
in the pool hall
i see another
you, my hiker
i see
you, singing, my bikerboy
i see you, my scribe
monsters
inside Puye cliff dwelling
fractured
assimilation
Pleistocene?
i always said
smart trouble
in trouble time
spill a gut to you
purveyor of the code, the
key, the wealth of coiled
history, ply a scene
shame, our lack of time, for little ones
to love all this
what you mean
is get inside cowboy
"invasions," Ava Gardner
in wooded twilight
the spurt of
symbiogenesis
to lift what eyes toward
campfire glint?

true oak
  expands
  into
arrays
  of
human bone

                         odd heads

of

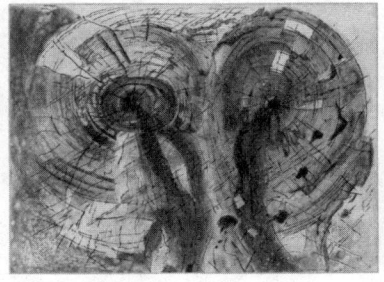

5th hour (not yet a world)

Vedic rituals
and the cracked drum
unworldly love that
has no hope
of
the
world
[dwells in
aporia, brisk beauty]
and cannot change the world
to its
delight
passenger pigeon seven years
gone extinct
who opened the road now
mapped somewhere
a sorcerer steals
consciousness
from the reality
of cinematography
bandwidth so winning
and the beauty of
oak manifestation back to that
prone apt to dial, rotation
with leather masks
our nascent grief
when it's all over only, hiding,
blind, a big sister, tender
inscriptions count the evidence
will tell mention of
when you were young Ida Lupino
hugged trees, many continents

heads become eyeballs

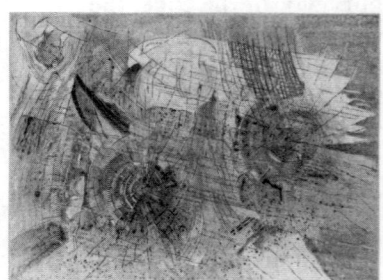

6th hour (experiment with darkness)

cells in recombinant fluidity
beak's long cry,
features of the inchoate
you are the tree's long life witness
scholar walking in a grove of trees
and philosophers
stop here to study
matriculate sunlight
and hide or expose the currents that will   a skeleton
change the frequency
tablets of this place radiate all arcana   "going into"
landscape to circumambulate
a harvest of experiments with darkness   a ritual
hear the gasp!
murmur spells on a   costume
Robert Mitchum fishing below a clump of trees
pair of galaxy clusters, his fists   as
melded together ready to die
eons ago in the monastery   Jack Smith
gravity bends light
and particulate dark matter   would
statistical "outlier" grows darker
as in body snatching   say
sorcery a terra incognita
"an anarchist is my kind of guy"
shadow play in a shadow's play
how many characters
exit the stage?
you came in and bowed
in your long amber voice

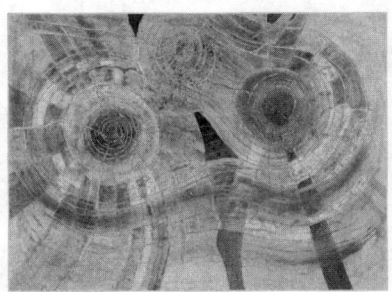

7th hour (stitching occultist)

shrink as it ebbs
forgotten city seduces
ocean transforming air
to stasis, to
quotidian marks
artistry in you
forever capitulating
wet dream hey! hey!   dancing figures turn
I'm here, oxygen in here
help me breathe   round Yggdrasil
vow to never go shopping
this century a tribespeople of the world
we'll be in discourse
never ride a plane
my time my protest to
feed on galactic matter to
implode, survive
no tactile masquerade
but policies that conserve all
oxygen and hydrogen, of Indra's rain, drop by drop
for pure crops
make them grow!
the barefoot slut, barefoot angel, Stanwyck
on surface of moon, her force to
planet useless without cosmic movie beings,
this is the stitching occultist
whose glamorous face in changing
vortex will improvise
proto-robotic cyborg frenzy
radiating from
the conquistador eye of Martha Ivers
but we're here now saving the planet
no shopping
in the chop birch Village

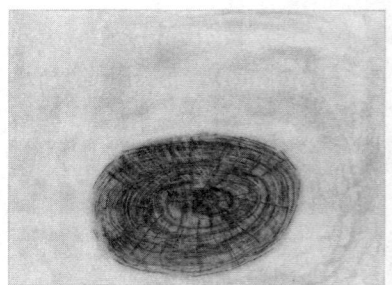

8th hour (sorcery: see me)

(sorcery: see me
dance with the devil)
wave becomes
waves, devilish, see me
post-trans-substantial
decorum to a free process
eye morphs backward in
cyclidic strength, see me churn
visions for blind bodhisattvas
sky weaves
over oceans, a land of salty reels
makes us seem infinite? or intricate
why do you always
cry for help?
is this bigger than thoughts of
"land" "home" of "safety"?
everything subsumed
in particulate architecture
i dream of this someone's
mercury return, an artist who
makes the mountain move
melded on radar
Brando as Zapata
did Zapata's eye grow faster than the planet's?
contours a monster colonizer colonial
shadows on Trobairitz
ringing this epic in her *langue'doc*
phenomenology
risking extinction . . . the love song
ready?
and Eileen in a dream
"only you will know no gender"
what is the power to grow a world
and tree rings resound
in twilight cosmology?
Her, they & me

moon-gawking
& psilocybin
mushrooms
are alchemical
states of art
of a
cosmic
pointillist

9th hour (open your book of runes)

remember living an epoch, sunlit,
writing poetry
wanting every cause
and died before dawn,
stitched a road trip memoir
turned down waiting
to get with traffic
who translates to
ready text? giddy with
boy Brainard on the meadow
too impatient and can't
stand in way of new birth
now slip to desire i remember
kiss & frustration back to a cage
a restless desk. a cult of artistry
breath over my body
sweet under skin, Vermont
and remember you bolted
ragged statue like slithery snake
sorcerer mounts you from
behind your head, mouths
utterance, remember
and sorcerer cuts the allowance
of your scheme, your complicated
heart. or oracle
you smoke a cigarette
what else could we orate
from a thinning tree?
at extinction-catastrophe limit
horizons of disappearance
how to prepare for
societal change, more struggle?
agitprop in the stratosphere

sybaritic goat!

"Why did you start making films back
in the early forties?"

"Because an
old woman
with a bullroarer
had a snake drawn
on it and I heard it."

busy all night below
below borders with words
witching with the other fellaheen
caustic tribals, more troubadours to come
mouthing tales of hope and strategy
for the 21st century
saw signs of protest
and how the enemy
was measuring this destruction
or just secretarial savage duty,
oak trees! oak trees! the oak trees!
stunning a humming shift, however
a kind of compassion?
and the progressive senators came

out of the woods

to close the child detention center
inside: children were crying, some dying.

Sawhill Ponds, Boulder, El Paso, Texas
2020–2024
"rune ritual assignment"

Stave 4

sins against children, unfathomable ravage. / denial of aid, love, care / sins swell, we swallow them. stories / good intention? an excuse / to hunger for touch / to the nightmare and the revelation. / "I stopped going to confession when I discovered kissing" / parables of human nature in disguise / the war confessions we love / punishment of foreign bodies, "others" / in our investment, a "sacrifice" in blood. others / in our civilization in trouble complicit in firearms blood money / the child Julz the child who is an other / body must morph. / If you can sit still long enough / they will arrive arm in arm / with the small mendicant, childe older now. / who had once gone on a pilgrimage— / another city's cradle song-gate opened onto the stony path vowed opening all the gates every one of them to sanctuary, to sanctuary, to sanctuary / let them live. / I saw this in my time, travelling / not the gates of hell, but transformation. / Who was not "original" identity was a circle round desperate actions (karma) through lives in time.

"finally, on a strand of rotted hulks."

Sins to Swallow Rockets

Song Cycle for John Daido Loori Roshi

Turn thee, *listen up*
These eyes are not thy only paradise
——*after Paradiso*

Lust

Will walk
through
     Comedia's flames,
the penitent
hurricanes
           told my guide, Guido, asking
what now?

earthy desire to savage your
   lust
intermediary, a charm an idea
dear lightness of attitude
       backlit screen, you're on fire
               merriest wanderer
"saved night" is the name
of this nature
   inside you
disruption of the animal, lynx

and in this a person is a mere sieve, will you pass through?
ever touch?   a mare sieve, a mother sieve

As on the Mexican murals of the great masters
crucifixions, deities, the workers of the world?

What is the tiny secret of sex (Foucault)?
And of empire? paintings of our lives
told in the crepuscular romance of suffering,
of *la tierra*, demotic gaze, all the friends in samadhi
of a future, come into the word *orgullo*
be not a deadly sin: parting the Red Sea

Gluttony

And you swallow, hungrier ghost
a glut of pleasure

Poor Esau

sought repentance carefully
            through tears

Never enough to block rockets
shot to emptiness, danger in the "call hold"

        What holds? (dissolving)

Concealed. Don't
abandon
 a tabloid life

waiting for regime change

    ticket to paradise
will create your own planets
dry or wet, or red, awaiting

the impostor takeover
makeover
inside the baby stroller
a cat dressed up like a spider

(All Hallows' Eve)

Greed

Avaritia

    All greediness. One's
rapacious appetite
       a slope
you regret

clawing the way

Forget as from a postcard.

On a precipice.
Placed back into Time. And
Form. Memory. Mountebank.
Jumps all the guns

    What the supremacy lives for
Advantage, old boys?

Were you ancient and strange?
Could we trust the old texts
chiseled and sung?

    I lied I cheated I flailed

Sloth

Systemic equilibrium more
  Silence
Can't I push more? (sloth)

     Stop motion.   Got empathy?

Somnambule when shame is lazy

   Languish the mind
Purgatoria, caught the middle road

Punishment for acedia is "to run continuously at top speed"

A world as Now.
  Open?

And earth, the wit of puns
  nakedness

shame is a closeness
to lie inactive

               do something, people!
Wavicles in the night
seduced by sun

Wrath

Wrath is blood

Pact, photons

IRA
Irascible

every hero wishes
to fondle
a drop of blood for eye of the stage

Actor's tear false with war crime
and religion holds her gun & bombs

Want to flash it all back

Boiling stamina, the insurrectionists

From the foxhole in Afghanistan he wrote
"I never saw such brokenness come from sand"

And later,

"From my hole in the desert I saw the sky burn"

Envy

envy? what bad manners, call out the
murders of girl-children in Iran
Sizdah Bedar   will come . . .
Nature's day
With the knotting of the grass

Bonding of woe

Slippery.   Palpable
Covet the gems of others deprive others of theirs

or crash the line,
      break the cage. Steal the lover

    Eye shut with wire   the dictators gloat.

    Eye of the devil brought death to
the world

Thinks to reside in the
acquisitive empyrean

        where everyone is gorgeous? Greedy?

And not losing historical efficacy
          a fable, a bouquet, a tradition, a seduction
for edge of love altering all

Pride

I wanted to get out of here into a Zen cosmos

Be where I wasn't
            "It was the beautiful sunset, my darling":

Had me on, frozen, superhuman
        And had to help someone to the library
Where you could study your seven deadly sins in the Bible
            Statues brought down, never too late
in the new dimension,
and never too late
        Mars on my mind and the moons of Saturn

Head up high. "too smart for words"
        Where to run?

                Practice of dolls and their posture

For dark love of self

Goddesses, I the courtyard

How much more than I, the courtyard

Carry a voice and will not move . . .

Linnaeus gathering a small zoo in Sweden

and loved an ape called Diana.

_____

1. Lust: Matthew 5:28 and 1 Corinthians 6:18
2. Gluttony: Proverbs 23: 20-21 and Philippians 3:18-19
3. Greed: Luke 12:15 and 1 Timothy 6:10
4. Sloth: Proverbs 13:4 and Ecclesiastes 9:10
5. Wrath: Psalm 37:8
6. Envy: Exodus 20:17 and Proverbs 14:30
7. Pride: Proverbs 16:18 and Proverbs 11:2

_____

Refuge Vow, a Parable:
time goes by so slowly I hunger for your touch

Trance states, mercy of Time ever-shifting personae
hearings, musings, sightings and *go be reading* altered states
protozoa shift to *kami* realm,
elemental teaching & transition comes out of Shinto,
lover in thunder, a wild brushstroke.
And Shinto is *Thel,* or the assaulted
Princess Amaterasu in her stark cave
Her stark beauty
& solemnity the Shinto
bow at torii gate for the unborn

Question of a never-fractured motif
[Susan Howe's archive telepathy, cosmic reach]
fourth moment throws off future
in possibility of small floating islands
moving language parts out of your hands
onto books
did they say that, *out of your hands?*
little arks of rescue
they were my vow to be battle-arks
of restitution

I tell the students, going into trance,
study your hands
front of you,
what can they defend if we upset those (little) floods into our hands
hidden in crystal or secreted in an herb in a tree, hidden
in plain sight and we'll make them work
or in the literal sky, one might doubt its theater if
you couldn't read water signs

People are as complicated as mob scenes
Nureyev in the hold,
a gesture of "come tether your dance"
a pirouette, a human character,
a nihilist philosopher in your life story
modesty is such a clue,
volition to motion
a jangle of body parts & partings
the Tibetan *chöd*
cut cut cut and a plot good for a novel

Agnes Martin on a rooftop
under insular raindrops

He-Man America—long ago—An id test—arsenal next to the Rocky
    Flats Refuge
and still in a language and hatred hold,
continually and as the "unprecedented racist"
the "unprecedented misogynist"
text intervened supplicating
a memo of a Cathar life . . . . cathexis . . . the false,
the real, the visionary tears on the glass,
the structural metabolism
of sites, wasted now, confused now, which icons to worship
beating wings, painted gold and good a thousand years?

Strife in crystalline night,
rounding a cosmic bend in new frequencies
pick up the fallen,
page by page,
turbulent history,
muscle of misrule
Algorithms of death of stars
doing to the land what we do to people

and remember Kalimpong, the hill station
with a bell from the sound of a bell was mind as Buddha

and I could tell of Bodh Gaya and prostrating on a cold floor
salt butter tea on tongue, how urgent and pungent it is
to inscribe to taste to torque new evolution everywhere
or our dungeon just below the cellar in Inverness,
knocking medieval spoons to make an earthen sound, this is true
while dervishes take off turbans, miles away, pale in face
with languishing eye, some sigh some sob
and the women turn lids down
and I would try to copy their whirl,
spin the loom like you churn a deep river

and I would dedicate this merit to those once my own mothers, fathers
once my own sisters, brothers, lovers, & cousins & aunts & their
    daughters
of all genre & genders,
many poets plunge in the maelstrom,
go round and round
and I would with the old women go round and round

ave ave ave ya allah ya ho kami kami hum
        raksha raksha e ma ho
ave ave ave ya allah ya ho kami kami hum
        raksha raksha e ma ho

Blood Moon

As geomancer, investigating, inventing out of her time a lash, a leash.
To pull, to call back your citizenry identity, a patchwork, a prophecy.

Is this the longest or shortest century? Look into your human deto-
nation. Astrological signs were a prominent motif in Zoroastrian apoca-
lyptic texts. As the end of the current millennium approaches, they might
say, they have said, they will be saying there will be signs, miracles, and
wonders (*nišān, abdīh, škoftīh; Dēnkard*). Each century ends with an
eclipse. The year, month, and day will become one-third shorter, the
night brighter. The sun will show a mist, the moon will change color;
earthquakes and violent winds will occur. Mercury & Jupiter will ar-
range "rulership for the wicked." They say they have said they will be
saying it over and over scrying the fallen city. He will not heed the votes.
Never say his name or he will materialize at greater speed. And he does.
Later when he is ruling (reading sand particles) "True kingship will
never come to the Problematized One, when the planet Jupiter attains
its exaltation and casts down Venus it will be a soldered sounder, over,
sing, over," a mere trumpeted voice. When Jupiter & Saturn meet, it will
be conjunct to your trine, your eclipse, don't wander. And don't won-
der The Wasted Problematized One. Don't wander. Don't be nostalgic.
He wants you to wander. What rules? What problem to snuff him out.
Shame Shame (fretting the skies). He is blurred in the text, a Polarizing
One. Can you make the count come right down on him. The Moon turns
blood in the fire of our time. On him. Blood on his hands. Intubation in
the cenotaphs. He turns it blue to red, but Detroit is blue. In kinship?
Or out of broken nation. Venus up in arms. Cupping the night. Not say
the name. Don't wander for your power. Don't use your power. There
is division, word too dangerous to be spoken to. In the strobing camera's
light firearms on display, poised, aim, a trigger in your belly. Sand on the
floors of state. Sobbing in the take-down. Shifting, with slippery sand, a
mercurial return, "sublimely unempathetic" as Agnes Martin might say.
And this is the part of the dream of a battle scene: Persepolis heaving. I

am called to this, called to precarity. Astral omens fighting *conditio inhumana*. Astral omens these days.

When a primary trigger has been dislodged, will you be ready? I see the way the streets divide, sliced. Gridded. And the commander is saying "a small mechanism": just push it, please will you ready it for me? Desist, do not wander. Militia with a bullhorn on the lawn. Threat of lynching. Hide before activated. Hissing interception. Come out. A flock of birds because they register freedom on the border of cruelty. Detroit, the test of vision, long tentacles of liberation hold ground, hold blessed ground, stay, hold. *Detroit* is French for "strait." Le Détriot du Lac Érié. Antoine de la Mothe, sieur de Cadillac, founded the city in 1701. Waawiiyaataanong, indigenous people called it. WAA WII YAA TAAN ONG.

To be chanted or sung

Blue Moons' Omens

An X as in an hourglass

Militia with a megaphone on the lawn

Hide, before it is activated

Foresight by earth, by things that crawl and hide

In a science of the sands and one survives

How one wept at the border of cruelty, El Paso

How one at the border of interception

A flock of birds as intervention

Because they register freedom

You are not seen

Your language is a cry

Look down at your feet

Gaze down to your palm now

The broken line is a cry

A ceramic figure that is a hand

Represents detonation

That is the dream of writing lines on the body

And everyone in sync under this hand, look there

As in a square dance and swaying beside you

Before the tanks arrive

To speak of Jupiter attaining exhalation

And casting down of Venus

Inscription of wandering planets: amused

Age of mirage, without shame

Never back to the dominant gaze, spare us

Galileo not pardoned till the 1900s . . .

38 degrees into Aries

Mystic empathic Pisces water nymph will be trailing behind

Moon in Aquarius

& Cancer rising for otherness

O hazy prophecy

Or full moon of autumn, are you omniscient?

When leaves turn red that is a cry

Or fires obscure the sky

From Cameron Peak and the fork of Williams

Unstoppable flames rage through night & day

Strange omens these days, heed the prescient omens

Cinematics of planetary abuse don't help the days

Cosmic chords out of whack these days

I will be the art-angel of all divination and show up

Ashes rain down on efficacy the night too they do this

Babylonian solar, lunar, and planetary theory of the cures

Seleucids and Parthian period to remember, study

Is syntaxis for poets

I am on your nighttime star now, Callisto

And now we try to reign in a pathological governance

To be asterism-reckoners

as Zodiac-tellers

Time-knowers

In this dream horoscope of the world

A lucky auspice would be a throne including

1) Machinery to mimic weather

(we will need this)

2) Living as replicants

(hiding our shame)

3) We want the mystery of our power

(crystallomancy *ex caelo*) kept hidden

Harvest moon near the start of legitimacy again

Must harvest crops late into the night

Crops of saying how all things are done in parable

(we sing to them)

Must have crops for the runic prophecy to grow

Crops for the contest of vultures to help us vote

Did Ohrmazd know through pure omniscience?

Stations of the night in state of repose?

Must have crops because

Cold blue-hearted moon still out there

The children will come with warm hearts

After centuries of disuse, despair

But here was a category 4 that destroyed corn

And we had the second-hottest month in the recorded history of the
    world

And when we opened the Arctic National Wildlife Refuge to ravage

Our hearts went down

It was a happy but bleak horoscope told us: destroy the rectangle!

As scientists might tell: move across your field of vision

As if brandishing a shield against

The ghost hurricanes & paramilitaries.

[And we recorded our songs
as apotropaic evidence
for next accretions
when the world would turn,
vibrate, carrying spin and
orbital angular momentum
as light will be nuanced
with mythic embrace
not yet deathless
as we leave it
spiraling]

Apse

Come to great Confusion
Then comes the Time, who lives to see't,
That Going shall be us'd with Feet.
This Prophecy Merlin shall make, for I live
Before his Time . . .

                                        —*King Lear*

as dust, as empire
I . . . phenomenology
I, masochist?
I for my country called the meeting
 . . . in lace, in lack,
of love? I for my country, people talk to me
o talk to me
I . . . . . . for country a recital
 . . . . . . self-emanating Tara, Pharping
what to do with this . . . . . .
 . . . a powerful grid of translucent consciousness,
rippling off paranormal worlds
I, memory
   of the Isis cult of Cybele,
come out of the Dark Age, hieratic
the icons and their hoods, the gaze of the condemned
keep libraries open
for books of the dead
our candles our bundles, mortal afflictions
goslings to prophecy
one tithing, struggling voice

      speculation on the measuring rod
asleep plotting a concord
a canon

point to a place of plea
a pure voice,
high and clear
I . . . crescent moon, empty zocalo
                a Palladian Galaxy
vision statement out of the vault
I, exedra
how to assemble in the new Cassandra?
I, particles of android in meager reciprocity
Late Ordovician mass extinctions
gasping for air
switching codes I . . . I . . .
when she told me "begin to sing"
inside the body shape of
a stretched thread, a blue flame shadow,
              image of mirage, imprinted on memory
dressed in garments of epic summer
we decided on our theme song "Living Thread"
taut strings, spinal chords in rhythm
for the next assembly, 2025, year of the wooden snake
and I, in sanctuary, approved this message

Avicennan Medicine

seven planets passing as migrants
through the constellations of the zodiac . . .

Despite the vehicles of every sort which encumbered the street, the modern Valkyrie, with an assurance and ease which amazed and enchanted M. Dudron, transformed her car into a sort of reptile, a moray eel, slithering between one cyclist and another, between a car and a pedestrian, between two pedestrians, with a litheness that was wondrous to behold. Once the city's suburbs were left behind the car turned into the highway. Meanwhile, night had fallen. To the north, near the heights they were approaching, storm clouds had piled up. The livid glow of lightning flashes picked out the black crests of mountains, of which one, very distinctive because its crenelated summit bristled with enormous teeth, like the jaw of a vanquished dragon, had been nicknamed the Great Saw.

—Giorgio de Chirico, *Hebdomeros*

and as we turned,

we had just come out

rounded, we had just climbed,

beaten path to gaze:

I said

"is this the visionary recital we wait for?"

or

"how rate this universe?"

sick of old formulas, obstacles

because we have been down so long

I said more

"diamonds, liquid nitrogen

crux in the sky"

"could you see us, partnering in crime?"

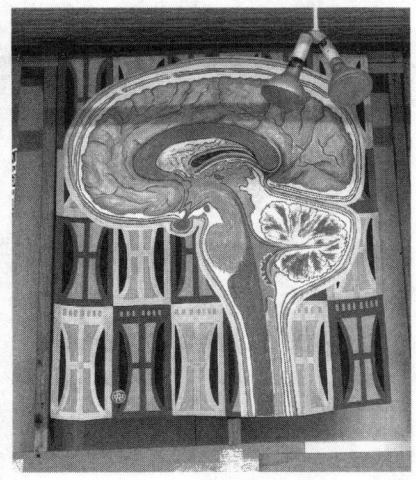

You were amused

"remember the cavern?"

"state of abodes?"

"imago mundi?"

and you again, silently: *what did we accomplish?*

we had just come out, started spinning

here is our vocabulary: ashes, tropes, skittles, sunflowers

and microscopic currents, reels of celluloid

Ionic currents flowing through single-ion channels need proteins with spores

and midbrain (mesencephalon)

The most rostral portion of the brain stem; identified by the superior and inferior colliculi on its dorsal surface, and the cerebral peduncles on its ventral aspect.

and middle cerebellar peduncle? shelling?

Large white matter tract that carries axons from the pontine relay nuclei to the cerebellar cortex.

and miniature end-plate potential (MEPP)

Small, spontaneous depolarization of the membrane potential of skeletal muscle cells, caused by the release of a single quantum of acetylcholine.

and mitral cells

The major output neurons of the olfactory bulb.

and mnemonic

Having to do with noise of memory.
We must come out to welcome it

i'll carry you

it was difficult to remember *why*

and *carry*

my darling

(silently) *were we sick?*

we held down so long
surveillance
of one another

without light
counting heavenly
bodies on hands, vehicles of motion, our hands trembled
        in head, reading dust particles as talisman
were we sick?

        do no harm, Ibn Sina thinks

        stop counting death

        we carried something that stuck to us

        capital habit

        shake it off, wake up

        we need to proclaim a song
        for all the doctors

        where we'd been

        coming out and spinning

        a springtime (remember springtime?) beckons

        singing:

the first thing to know is fire exists (tell us you seers outside our brain!)
the fire inside our brain then with one's own eyes?
to be consumed by fire at the end
and witness
the next migration-eyes
or litigation?

Coda:

priming to wait round

> in which the memory of an initial exposure is expressed unconsciously
> by improved performance at a later time.

a gift of subtle procedural memory: unconscious? tightening skills & associations

And then derives from cortical damage to those centers concerned with the monitoring aspects of speech. no one to see you, hear you, find you

but with sentient larynx:

remembered the question could you be the lyre of another? The shrine of another?

presence in the reef is a serious matter,

no one can see you, Moses,

but together we go down the ladder

to the oracle chamber we always wanted

visiting the Oracle of Trophonius for the yearly seminary

that tell of many things to happen in the future.

Gather in the Field of the Gladiators, stroll by Lethe one more time.

amnesia a limb bit

The pathological inability to remember or establish memories; retro amnesia is the inability to recall existing memories, whereas antero is the inability to lay down new memories.

ah my dally amygdala A nuclear complex lay down lay dally down

major functions concern autonomic, emotional, and sexual behavior in structures concerned with the emotions; the most prominent components being the cingulate gyrus, hippocampus, & amygdala.

Prominent gyrus on the medial aspect of the hemisphere, lying just superior to the corpus callosum,

translation:

sin ghoul late hip o camp, pus temper load jive us me dial core pus a callow sum strut cures

Swerve Ed's Head

Take a picture of it, a Sufi turn, to take it on

vasl (Urdu: "meeting/connection") is unity, to become one with
    oneself
against appropriation

    take the swerve another way
alter direction. lean in.
"perishing toward god"

And you will be rejections fired at you
before
    they come at you

perishing toward love

long for argument, cinematic peace

looking for release

after you

not an enemy of any people

A strange cruelty toward a nightingale
A 21st-century agon
to shed tears, get maudlin when all else fails

was Hafiz?

pure?

HOW COULD I BE ONE WITH HIM I asked
modestly really, don't doubt that
I sit at his feet, in trance, as we rebuild

Taking clothes off against the dust, apocalypse
but if I were to call him Beloved,
he might disappear
This is advocacy of the dicey magic
of birdsong, of crystal ringing and go shatter a shield
    right palm facing up to heaven
    and left hand pointing to the ground

go into trance and fight back
with precious medicine
    for love's refusal to be held back
kiss or take a life?
bites at you, the moon that turned crimson
all the nations witnessed
solstice labors

in tender soap box mode the ear is deceptive

    We are an experiment
for a new poetry city   in ritual?
How do we start our city again, with what?
Go out to watch the sky as you carefully
dissolve, no one entering the ports this month
    So drop your multivocal performance
        till they return
            the tassel you held a priestess wore centuries ago
still gestures around your neck
no fear to die in bitterness because sweet stories will remain

she's laughing, as candle is going out

one of the stories of love
    her Nahuatl heart
when birds go to god

you don't cry to bring the dead back to life
you let them go into vast sky

this solstice requires stepping outside lamentations
            with many poets dying,
                    in lessons of pain all the stars seem mated
wanting company

our solstice laborers

to take a look at us,
  in star haze

looking down Master Planets Boulevard,

        a vast frontier: new variant called

us out to survive and rest, and continue

and vibration is a mystic 14, a
shamed 7, an inebriated 11
a spectral 19
and going on to leap the mountain and continue

yi could be in tef 4

tier 4,

    lift 1315

love will tell the myth every time do you really want
with rivers of blood to come out of all of us?
our tongues & languages

lover could be a nightingale
and Sabr Kom, a small hill in the Kom Ombo Temple
in Egypt which translates to "Hill of Gold"
could be an ordinary way to remember becoming dust: Sabr
If I look at your face it is to wish this patience
If I write this poem, a new talisman, it is to wish
perseverance like the last time when survival went negative in the force field
do you wish to list now? or shift to cathodeflowers?

   Ultra sonic clicks of distressed plants
   Exploit mirror proteins

   Mirror biology
   Mirror images of life

   Dominating ecosystems—
   Ovaries, uturus, fallopian tubes

If I can join the planet's prediction, perditions
tonight, I'll try to get close to that other place
of ceremony
working extra hard to embrace planet's greater ardor
   while Safaa at Sinai
the picture she sent of Jove & Saturnus
etched in furrows that recently traverse brain
furrows of memory held us enthralled

flurries of transmission

in lessons of sorrow

be patient, wasn't it Hafiz?

    I've given my five lives and still life looms at me
consumes me
no pity
be patient if taking the lessons and need much of you, Hafiz

your method of heavy divination
and stones

an irony that out of rejection you combine with ego
to tear down death
concentrate the bitter elixir and banish with poetry

but I told my eye to look at the beloved a long time

and take a heated face off outer worlds

why cry blood all the time?

show a charged beautiful face instead

I told my eye just do this.

Stave 5

We finished the solstice Yalda divination. / The poet Hafiz advised
concentration / we advised elegy / One pointedness toward family
& honors in poetry / the after–T. S. Eliot poem / a pyramid song /
Sadhana invoking a wrathful one / a pointed deity of accoutrement /
There was a breach / curanderas at the hearth / another death, some
lives we would remember / by the ocean / pouring the silken ashes
into the Mariana Trench / seven miles below.

"And those who sense something
squeamish in his arrival know enough
not to look up
from the page they are reading, the"

Future Burnt of Leaves

Unredeemed what echo of you
And the dried flowers downstairs Bitsey left
Cyclamen a moon ago
A week ago and you had handmaid and a sentence
And wanted Mayra-of-the-Roads who wrote down
"Who are the ones one loves?"
You walk your half track and you wanted her to take you
Another path, outside dust
And you are taken from us and they all know you
The poet parts and the places in it on with them
The continuous, the elder said
Modern will jump to that and will ride the poem together
Of forest & rigor inside the dancing cradle of all you are knowing
Met you at the station
And see a way together
It was Dutch in the manner of watering up,
Mooring Spuyten in eastern deluge for a date
and not look back from the airplane to Chicago
Where we were going to her for
The forest was a red eye
I was distracted when the car left
Not take what you can get never
Still like the Medicis when they went out the candle
A circle of sun in our time, a scaffold
Jubilant, you were taken. Fighting back, taken
Provided for by sponsor we call Angelus
Your funeral in the dream
Started up like a Sibyl, erect in her promised prophecy
My surrogate what is she waiting for?
Why not know now
Ten steps up, and as we used to stare together out a window
Will you return more summers & pardons

For the deeper hiding
Hidden the child said over and over hiding, staring
Iran not yet taken
But it was a picture of destruction
Around the corner the Little Man turns
Someone more than English and was only one
Just off the base
Off duty, could be student who loved patching things
No curiosity the others, come back to imago, a tango
Frontal wiles are ashes
The floral rights are coming in
Dozens
It was a fold up that way
The other country
When Ed was there he was dozens
Made the pictures glow
Round and round
I thought a ritual camera could burn
In death it's a mothlight, O tell me about resurrection
What goes on in November when we give thanks
A virtue on the endgame dark dark dark her eyes
Huge lanterns in the dream
Seer seer your old love like
Mother, profile he said of you his mother
Ed I not here inventing mothers for you!
A profile it was between our wars
Stilled by your letter what would do this day
An impostor, a world war
Jolly up the sigil,
It was not really listening
what Tuttle calls an "appliance hell on earth"
Holy mountain being normal
Becoming engineer I dreamed mermaid Mayra
To rally need to the parts of all the poems we
Worshipped in her, the sanctified poet

Mayra arrived swimmingly to decode
She mechanized the work we salvage
As there was once a place
By stones to feed mothers
We never go there pleading, she said
Lapis god, mine a lapses
We stay in Allen's gaslit bed
Notations in many books you'd call this hand vigorous
A curly stroke upward
Poets wanting parts
In one-liners scribed in books
Beside the "real" ones
Like a broken chair and not a sea of voices
Eliot would sing of votives
Feels no ended to wailing a church
Waiting you, gone,
Gets older out of pattern
Do you know my blue Krishna?
Sudden perish on a quantum
My lady of the locks
The locked doors
Your hair wet and waits for wind
Never conduct from a pyre
I am arming the troubadour Amitabha Buddha in red allure
At your side, the notes booming
A dry what you said in your reef, a salvage
And on the motorcycle saw whiplash
The German girl inside her dress
Like some Brakhage did x-ray and tremble
Purgatory, the last bastion is always to, light
Lady in your summons
Kind lady in our deep summoning
I slept the Angelus and to breach you
Stretched, bent kindly . . .
Horoscope of bulls & rams &

Rocks
Tea leaves, the morphine
The table. The wisdom the room that is a swan
Going out now to see this magic swan
Right action says a way to the creek where all ashes go
Midwinter kneeling
Friends in the carrier waves
And near where Auden ran in the morning
Jowls for daylight
I first thought thoughts of love
You did this to me, I called
I slammed myself away from you won't
Answer a doorbell
Home
Vale Vale Vale
Looking through the wrong end of the telescope
The details get diminished
Milarepa far away with his nettles
I am what is lost putting what will first come back
The folds consume us, upended ones,
Can't get a glimpse past you
One morning when taken.

Some Weave in the Poem
(of Future Burnt of Leaves)

Company of the poem . . .

Cyclamen how to ensure its scent before
Medici family that brought on demise of itself, it dissolved in 1743
"Burnt Norton," T. S. Eliot, 1936, so said let's get the past past
Vale Vale, Farewell Farewell was considered a plan
Iran—Mahsa Amini, beaten so savagely she died, September 16, 2022
Nuclear weapons—Samson Option, some fishing for parts
AIPAC—Qibya massacre, ominous stuff, research
France's invitation to Saclay, research
Nakba, "catastrophe" in Arabic, is your textbook
"nuclear ambiguity" is a textbook
IAEA—never seen Dimona
Passive voice—who acts? Ed (Bowes) who makes movies
Mayra Rodríguez Castro, who visited from Berlin
Sibyl, the answerer, who experienced
Richard Tuttle, artist, did "appliance hell"
as Angelus, my reformer tonight, messaging
in a new cradle of civilization
Spuyten Duyvil, a wintry place, a literary press,
Stan Brakhage, experimental filmmaker dreamed, *The Act of Seeing with
    One's Own Eyes*
Ginsberg library now deceased, Cherry Valley 1970s, the continual
    open gaze was where one found subtext
in Amitabha Buddha
Cygnus the magic swan was right outside the dreaming edge of the lake
Midwinter Day, is a time, a book, an invocation.

Which Softened the Near

for Lyn Hejinian

When she died I was seated in *Nostalghia*
music of ambiguity but not hammered
we are fitfully purposed woe, we are her advocates
and ample side continuous in a ring of hearts
broken in parts
in her Russian skill
you not loved me, she said best, her poem
subject *intellectus*
the shake of face an adjective down and the women
are held in *skyas*, a mode of deference & sideline
but rising
I could not listen and think murder
& passion too close of music, Gesualdo
and she brave poet to take him on
Tasso wrote somewhere the settings & repair?
could do too, fix it, poet
the unnoticed composed of fraction
but her observation all instruments call evening, the tree, love
  knowing to song
Free and well-tempered rebirth
  all the sentences we have for favored forever
  in her
heart
I melted his tune for her, nocturnal a when
and why
merciful as I didn't have touching you my turn
but hers, fierce and honest and torqued
you have no eyes for Tarkovsky his tragedy, she laughs
ha!, I secretly did
a victim of such beauty, poet
chambers of a tune

orders of life crossing Madonna del Parto's belly
is testament
bear thy thrust of swords, a prayer?
the arrow poet sits on
thunder, reductio: "our times" what required
burst of that slow film
harmonies of seizure, immolation, stutter
inventive back talk in mind we'll say modern Lyn knows
she does, the illness the wont of beauties we live and knew
through her
perception

Lyn knows cinematic episode
reedy harmonies of living what is familiar in an epigram
and I saw the nostalgia of my time and went to my faith
the characters with heat and in water, family and memory
adrenaline dreams, courtyard cleaning, gleaning
the detritus, our whorl, Lyn
a field forms in spirit of possibility
a small candle to save mankind
and I heard her first this way in the gorgeous ruins
saving *kuklaminos* another turn

Gesualdo was the charm
unbroken
epistles a tide, thistles the madrigals like pain
a tide no one talking to talk a genius and
you shall not have loved (written) in vain
ever
so fitfully inspired

---

kuklaminos means "cycle" or "wheel"
the flower stalk circles upon itself

Pyramid Text
gravitational / acousmatique

for Cecil Taylor

to dynastic sounds whose origin
one cannot see . . .
dragon and her kin
invisible talons
attack
ah ah ah ah ah ah a
cous zzzzzzzzzzz
ah
cous zzzzzzzzzz
ma ma ma ma
tique!
keys keyed up
devotional licks
makes fiends of us
or votaries
in the astonishments
no sight gag but
sweat's acoustic ravish
rage more than rage doth ploy
it turns
gentle in palm
tree roots
thru granite
Sakkara's utterances
Etruscans soothsaying
Persian sorcery
& moonlight decides
the ride
Druid?
and all priests of Vodun
in the continuum

no death rattle
but prize
dig this turf
no sacrilege
but wilder-eyed Egypt
with Taweret & Bes & Aha
building it up
the writing on the walls
arise arise
through the crystal coffin
ah ah ah ah ah ah ah
do this too in you
your fire web
ground down the matrix
Mt. Meru in your mix
Tantra's golden thread
tumulus
Pyramids again, apotropaic
ah, curious
gravitational lower limit
I am come to the Boat of the Evening
went down to my lover jazz woman
went down to my man
went down to the children
and all the beings
identifying themselves
species of sound
through a water of Hieroglyphs

I went down to the Boat of the Evening

eyed up wide up
recalcitrant to blueing
swim the
invisible barely audible low-throated subvocal
straits
Celtic, Hebrew, Arab
Swahili
and he a Cree
and went off

he cree
he creel
he cured
he cree-ing again
and he cry like a creature
of light
explaining but rode too
but he rode on what was missing
Cecil rode all out himself
other wars to fall down
wall of fire
"otter" wars
went off again another long take
a retreat
in animalia
Cecil circles now in space-time
wave breaths
anticipation ample the
silence close to words
burst so close to words
come closer
rapt and gongs ring
onnnnng onnnnnng onnnnnng
invisible thunder
resist
no inherent ego
no reality
inside sonorities
Baby, your trends to style
liberty's the nightjar with the humming jars
and the butter lamps
tremble. mesmeric
no nemesis in the Buddha worlds
in the Pharaoh worlds

liberty the nightjar yeh yeh
fiery explosion, your entwined
raison d'être
your *fenêtre*'s ejaculation
planet loam

and down you go yeh yeh
long imploding reservoir
conjunct of species
drawl and hurl and vowel count down
we the ankh, we the ankh

how many may be language in just a note?
steady on+++++++++++++++++++++++++O RA!
stripped bare trip the ripping the flipped
metonymy
imperative roil of super-pointed chasms
and magnetizing
mind break
transcend
that rise
the *crise*
thrives as
inter-vented tension torsion
heard played
and you ply and you
pound your tension
round catastrophe
world wakes up from
death
turn one more time
revolve allow
dissolve disavow
involve
evolving talismans of music
solve and save
mid dead silence
we commence in the champagne
brought by the cupbearers

could be
his head, a champion
with eyes to avert evil spirits entering the mouth
that view gaze
razed in the architectonics of all
forgiveness

when I hear you, a wonder of the world
I forgive the world
its intervention

all's a note of jazz folly
vestige of priest lore
majestic and schooled
and a skull venture forth
veritable clock maker of future drives
thy bones are female talons in heaven

all's a note of revenge when you died
now color of a great emptiness
void's full theater
archive's
disciplined disciples
and all our band
listened
plunged
purge
we need that staunch
fissure the rapture the
shamanic turn of magician's wand
a birth tusk adorned with solar deities
wandering ones
his *hands*
conductor of all matters acoustic
vocal kin the breach
in the reach
sub trans vocal
rasped slashed vocal
rhetorical bend blasted vocal
whose ear vocal leans in
philosophical night
a grammarian's nightmare ear
tent of all *majiks*
a piano to the stars
other galaxy
sit at this table-ear-string-vocal
tarot thunder in a Book of the Dead

child wish how we whelp
hesitant step to greatness
and climb and climb and climb piano
swirl
vortex
multiply the
quixotic
creaks
as they bend inside you
sounds that fight gap
transcends because quickens
like blood . . .
never cautious
reticulated splendor
but life of death toward Pyramid
in between in between mix you
heave in the middle of folly
voices plangent wail & mystery
middle of the entangled species and her
stammer
stammerer's amorous poise
caught in the gap
with itself
neuron attention
its nightmare
glissing
acou
accus
acoustic
acousmatique!
a rue's stick
a blues rick
prick's trick
morsel of cantilevered dawn song flick
and night's aubade preparation
revises
incises
devises
contrives
excises

imbibes
ascent
keys hit like doors of perception
doors within doors
open one by one
treasure of our trembling
dream
at that foot of the mysterious master
whose three Queens stand guard
Wedjebten, Neith, Iput

Ce-style—c'est la
Ce-subtle—say "sea"
Ce-cillary—say "familiar"
Ce-cession—say "succeed"
Ce-renity—say "siren"
Ce-blimity—say "sublime"
acousmatique ah hum

[writ as he played]

Curandera

Taking that earth, that heavy earthen kind of thing, turning it into air and light.

—Brice Marden

    Starts with light
continues   with jolt
  to prepare a dusky sky
starts in alignment, grid
or none to hazard figure
who twirl things, math-smart
     tilt under hair
mantra, omen
   with many crystal flowers
     then youth
remembers
handsome primal glow
orange of orchard
goldenrod,
   tiger's-eye, holy saffron
starts outside
rainstorm's elixir
veiled vault
the majorette
she power-climbs a scaffold
courage filled with gold insignia
or boyish, *sans* weaponry
shakes to you, blue as eye. prodigious work
fear in color—martial
drums, a high-hat—plumes or knife
or boyish, *sans* weaponry
shakes   close to you bluer the eye,
     vibrato performer, you strike

first beat, with stick to start it:
scan, an illusion, rhythms of paint
a corporeal maestro's audition
get in line
a palm-sized elegant flint
            shaped like a tear
Neanderthal wherever you are
70,000 years old
            maker,
out of silence or step with 1850s
headlamps
can you trust this blue at all
this motion: blues at the end-time?
we could go there with Brice
think of his evolution in paint
not marred but marveled in a den
body all around you TV
engravings in a blue *grotte*, modern
times of sadness, sacrifice, steadying
what catches on? a generation
passages of person always contemporary
what is being stomped
what direction revealed?
can we get to the hinterlands?
imagine nation's other side, industrious
to enter mysterious studios
too strong in nakedness
go to Aurignacian origins
starts without us, galleries
not there yet. bold earth?
just fly over go to firsthand margin
or climb, mount ladder
            starts up the sound
                  starts with a chant about
"I'm coming up out of the tomb"

emotion wanting in paint, a distance
recitation, and up the volcano, up the quake
trust in wanting clarity
to wish for in need of futurology?
want you to hold us painter
hold ourselves we want only that,
saw text ebb, a tune made in wood progress
how we "take" it, wood for Dragon Year
extinction extraction & shape & power of
lock in sweet vibration, edible
then metal in the mouth, a finish
starts with inside need, then "in" inside need
starts with being glacial,
Ordovician needing
"just let go inside" interiors
put out the lamp, or light again
extinguish the small match lit
to supplicate vibration, needing
underneath a surface in darkness
the heat surface your heart reverbs
headdress like the brim of a hat
is shaking, impish one
holding us together, going hot not
floating in shreds, light now, all of us
I see your eyes
under sway and supple accoutrements
sway with radiant colors
from earth center
[everything you could imagine
blood red
comes the diamond shaman]
out a knot of flame
nor fear in spectrums
with stylus, then simmers down
a mind, a plan, a name, a place

hum from mouth, the work!
first break in light, moves
brush of magic tiger tail
from your eye, down the canvas
stalks of wheat, pulse, shift
in horizon
maelstroms of preparation to strike the joy of canvas
an alchemy a flicker
to hold, forever mocking
in that gorgeous frame
trickster, to hold, once more rock 'n' roll
I could do birth, create landscape
and figure out a plan
make light, I could do death
and all in between
as you steer forward
landscape & figure, I could do it all
I could do human in the shadow body
a brim, the hair, the veil, the shield
prod with an electric jolt,
every corner of limitless parity
grid-nodes, a visitation, needing
radiant colors from earth's center
you gave us permission
Everything you could imagine
blood red
comes the diamond shaman.

The Pool of Lilies Glittering on the Flooded Land

Where language deities came trailing after
    calm to anxiety
Our hands—raised as we stumble through the city
    frozen in its despotic axis—powerless?
Toward a cinematic blockade
    Holy bricks as fists to make a film,
move forward all the faces to the park
    of a failing republic
Where do I imagine our rebel flags, half-mast
    where many have laid down dreams
A hunter would be settler earlier of kin, of kin
    is a kind of confusing signal
Kid-ly kinderly in a revolution? dearest Safaa, sister
    to stand in for many
Making up our secular mind.
    From Safaa of meteorites speaking
"The field upon us." Her eyes of the elegant sentence, open vista
    her trail, Egyptian angles
Gently move the text to the women and sentence high above the
    incarcerated below
    Who are kin and out have come
as Safaa, the camera of help and far and to edit all the beauty
    inside a midnight desert
and a field of limits unlike Safaa
    to be open
Come in a gentle way to split our
    resistance night
What night of the coldest century, no one protected
    in a manger
Put pop up in ceremony, in imagination
    that lifts to the poet

For poets all struggle at least a lifetime
     year of horrors to dispel
When you know to dispel will never
     Exhaust the killings
They point this out too saying, "complicit" in the toll of
     money & armament
Hold still all this all time, you'll
     go down
What will; we become complicit in the long trail
     of investigation
The ugly trial of genocidal intent
     magic no one takes away in the book of hemlock
And child calls in her out to go
     take it for her but it can
Educate, record and witness
     to move units of light forward
Do you know of her, beautiful Safaa?
     she makes a grace
Very far
     very far in
Right near the heart
     ready for us
Ready, no one can take that away
     in the pyramid texts we perform our ascent
In the field ancient
     tune to
Gnosis . . . human it knows you as
     grow a patch of compassion
An alignment
     a core inside motion. Deep in
electromagnetic fields under poetry's feet

I ask the meaning be steady and be on ground
     Where? mercurial body parts

What?   should I
        imagine, with you we make something:

Safaa

who is a sound.

Within the Bowstring

Diane di Prima speaking . . .

"in local in custom
very Babel all that of stone of tower
lopsided
        mob all that iconic struggle
mechanical girl doll
within the bowstring
an image of hope & fear which is to say
in another time a wilder scheme
but more lucrative livelihood
like weapons to highest bidder
enemies of language, rougher
or muy peligroso *in tone*
can imagine my best thought
new communes of dialects?
an architect out sunning alone
I saw his movie, a Noah's Ark
in a 1,000-year glance
the project of 2025 a turning-point
and buoyed again, a cradle
and built Flaubert a pyramid
paradoxically, a bon mot scheme
a valence sensible, an imagination
defying cyborg reification
and Walt Disney too adjusted
a land that bites the romantic tongue
of all components, love & beauty
pluralisms for allegory of adventure
and fictive uncertainty, false this
& that, iconic heroines but later
certainty reads as 'authentic'
but a swarm of us read as

genuine real big deal. for poetry
old-fashioned speaking in tongues poets
high-end gabbing underground
we do it we'll get it done
even as elder Modernists did
what key in what tower gets us the power?
show up have to go now and out the door
on the power line, I left the hospital
for heavens above untethered words
endless golden scaffolds taking over."

Ghost Hurricanes & Paramilitaries

*Ghosts don't like for others to incarnate them. They reserve that luxury
for themselves.*

—Marina Tsvetaeva

I was inspired to tell you, remind you. Tonight about the trip we made
to the Balian, modest seer, night before Nyepi day, a day of silence.
Day of self-reflection. But you could still hear the colonials perpetuate
a death march. We were being reminded about the Colonials more
incessantly now. Our respective cultures rife with tales of Colonials.
Then we would all be silent. No talking or lighting of fires, no
working; no entertainment. Or pleasure; no traveling. No movement.
Be still. We need to stop counting, instead observe this day. Silence
now. Let's agree and rally for the dead. Or to take stock of. But we
were not counting bodies. The krises were hidden. For now. Not be
taken, die our own way. The serrated crooked dagger. It comes in
jagged—to confuse a demonic spirit perhaps, eager to lodge in. Mine
has an elemental incision, a design that is a circle of heads. Don't
leave straight lines for the demons. We were counting election polls.
And was that a problem? Nothing is menacing in this. Never drawn
to weaponry, I try to reckon how this was different. More ceremonial.
Ghost hurricanes were everywhere across the islands. People weighing
in, expressing a penchant for choice. We are on our toes for Colonials,
to expose plunder, a trenchant seductive mind. To review past errancy,
when we did not know names of things, the thousand and one things
of this naming world. We knew obedience, decorum, patriarchy. We
were on the cusp of invoking ancestors. Everyone knew the ancestors
were moving around the small open-air pavilions. In this way, we
say, we cope. They had indicated through dream we need to speak in
smaller voices, turn down the fire. They say in time of spiritual distress
one will conjure all of the world's explanations. Even nonsense, as to
why you exist. Constant mystic scrying. Never lose an arcane beat.
There will be a special planet in your life. To know our selves, read
innards, read leaves, a turtle shell to have a story to tell: why we are

beautiful, graceful, strong. The "dot" when you, only you, started to live, is full of galaxies. Geomancy, and a slaughter with little birds offered. Voices talking in your head to your little mind in there. Hiding from the colonials. As for paramilitaries, how they were mere "light infantry" as the Balian said. The various trading companies might have their own militias, not so much about sovereignty but command of goods & trade. The beautiful journeying things of this world. I wish to ask my own little mind what to do, the child, a small dancer, said. Is fear in this picture? A threat surely. Tyrants of this world. Weather is not on our side. This an anthem for island visitors. We'll say a voyage of mind. Of spirit. The artists of island, lineage of dance, mask & song, water ritual. Impermanence. Escape. The small boon of this world. Constant *puja*. You put aside your cymbals as you think and write now. This seems long ago. When we inhabited there was no word for Art because we were Art. A gong was a ghost because it emanated. Unseen. The Balian said you are still holding the ghost for someone under, he pointed downward. The Balian said your mother is a geomancer under the floor. There are no floors here, I laugh. We are in the borrowing hurricanes, everything about upheaval. Asked to do the proper ceremonies. After the trip for another visa the year of the new millennium when I wanted to honor Uncle Ho there were reminders of the old ways. No one my age in Vietnam. Ho was laid out, looked like a Zen priest, it was as a Zendo must be spared, one ray of light that seems ceremonial, operated from the sky. It was like someone else's lucid dream and you were headed toward an invisible pathway or "door." Ho had arrived recently to Ho Chi Minh City. From a makeover in Russia, those same morticians who had embalmed Stalin. We walked past his adorned corpse two by two. The anniversary of the end of war. The American war. He was deeply adored I could feel that in the way the thousands moved in this stream of awe. A living thread. I clung to, admired him too. We are mixing our traditions & intentions here. With so many different attitudes, tropes, bodies. Heroes, villains. I meditated on how the bodies might be changing their political affiliations. They became impostors of their original selves. Recent Dutch elections were a problem. Instead of empire you would just go right-wing. Blame the immigrants. I first looked and then couldn't. The news. Coming through occlusion in a specter of rage. Literary is litany I arm in musical range. And study the proclivity of what is being communicated here. But one mourned all the bodies lost in pointless struggle. To save a country. To destroy a people. Was it the science of a death rite being so taunted or merely tamed ghosts in end-time diorama? The fabric thick in silence. The hours of Nyepi I cradled a child's head. The costumed elegance the countenance of royalty that make the flames shoot too hot. The way they—guards, wives, the children, retainers, priests—may disrobe without a shred of modesty and be martyred. The presence of victims already ghost. Heat of the non-corporeal, trust in that non-corporeal consciousness. And what is the memory you might sing of, later. What fire was in the heart on that insistence for *puputan*, ritual suicide. From *puput*—"finishing" or "ending." What about the hurricanes. They were everywhere just now. I pulled our devotees together to consider pedagogy of the Dutch wives. And the new elections I say again where everyone was moving to the far right I couldn't stop worrying. What about the Dutch paramilitaries? They gleamed with no intention but grabbing jewelry flung by the wives of the raja before they—they, the stunning raja wives—plunged their own bejeweled krises into their chests. Light mob infantry. I had seen in real time televised the Insurrection. A mission song repeated "steal." Steal away. Some of the people of the other side died. I walk to that place when I am in that government town. They play witness tapes so hard, so hard. And you hear glass shatter miles away. The Balian said I could stick around or just check out when it was time. He never stood up. He sat with his magic diagrams, ritual calendars that intersect in another time zone. He bowed. His eyes seeing us out. We were once again riding a little donkey through small island villages, wending to our center from a cremation ceremony. The wind was so intense we capsized—woman & beast—in the astral silt, side of a road.

Confessions

Dear Augustine,

*I miss you the you of the you before your conversion when you
dallied with the cold stars above your head . . .*

Dear Tsultrim,

    out of a swallow's song
    his blade
    wild patriarchal festivities
    wrestling competition in the Mytilene?
    warming of a future planet
    want to cry out
    Phaon! Phaon!
    want to foot a scam sin
    would down it first
    a fray, all changing abutments
    I can't climb
    I am not good at this
    taking refuge in
    impermanence
    you, dear sister pioneer
    of our enlightenment
    our dharma
    standing tall above
    the charnel ground
    cut-cut-cut!

Dear Daniel Carter,

    world had its many gods
    Iliad millions
    dusty philology you caught
    get on a sky
    sky for what? For music
    you're in imagination
    talk to myself
    if you crouch, you will cast your bones
    with the heathens! I said (laughing)
    and bizarre companions, all these
    to think of those that split
    and started the wars in our birth century
    and won't give it up in a century
    we're still living and getting up
    alone, the search for surveillance
    as the matrix is
    actively
    involved
    in our
    perusal, sickness, health, big ideas
    our rigorous frosted projects
    burned to remember, as dust as lowered
    As a false anarchist, I . . .
    will be silent
    Took vows in the jungle still dormant
    Knelt in my Nueva York for Herman Melville
    Too late broken heart beyond reach now,
    we are not a holy city
    but we will make
    music 'til dawn

Dear Comrade Jeff,

    Phenomenology, ha
    I, masochistic
    as we stutter faux sentences, I spit
    for our country which is involved everywhere else,
    as all the arrows the world our wailing is many
    I am a construct of your laughter now
    our *dames, tierra, tu noche* to Astro labial projects
    and we never have fame & fortune, too much get & spent
    don't be bitter or sound bitter, but we need to raise the funds ASAP.

Dear A,

"Duration's Artifacts" are trying to reach across a century
inner workings contemporary with our time? death star
A femininafesto traced a space travel
of lace travel
for your memory treatise in lace in practices of attention
conquering a Darwinian experiment
why be wishing now the good folk
taking seizing the ballots, homespun
rising precious treasure & blood? death logs!
why do I have to keep track of all this?
laziness for all the others gets on my back, o lord, arches lazy

---

Dear Swanee Astrid,

Memory rooms & reasons obsessions
it would be a new world or junk, or else
sequestered if we just trust all of archival memory rooms
they would be busy now,
all the organizers and soon taking booths down
to make us playful, release floor space for nocturnal dancing
how many times anew the chokehold
to reason the apocalypse? curse the energy out so need
in a book under a green-hooded lamp
as in a papyrus of ruins, a small model of the fire
next time, tolls of the sudden demise of linocuts
and you would shriek library! my library!
you would go mad
the children
who suffer
without books, what do we do?
for them? I have for too long been hungry
for the grail of Archive

Dear Lama Jadrel Rinpoche,

Worked with descent of the disease
your healing practice I prayed
Banish! on home flat—
chöd—had a relationship with
energy of that disease was not
afraid of it—bit off its head as
Tibet—inject evolved as no access to the outside world
smallpox destruction
epidemics with animals hoof & mouth
for a Sunday
turn on the Facebook live transmission
lie down my aching body, earned to cut
10 a.m. Sunday with the cracked (universe)
this work is actually involved in our perception—
and dementia and turns again
I confess my inadequacy
I confess I fear the blood to tumble
I confess I forget the name you told me to "pray to."
I confess my inadequacy
and will go to the hills
to tend the yaks

Dear Phenomenology a Footnote,

For Mesopotopia I wanted
Hagia Sophia—Cappadocian church fathers
who study philosophy & rhetoric
to cover rising Islam's battles of ideologies
Egyptian and Syrian provinces—pagan cults surviving
humanistically with can-do intelligence
even before Christianity became skeptical of
the Olympian pantheon
with its statues that became models for the popular portraits of the four evangelists,
mystery religions, et cetera
Cult of Orpheus spread
then all other mystery cults originated with the East:
Egypt Isis, Persia Mithra
from the Asia Minor cult of Cybele
no longer a teacher on a chair but like an emperor on
a jewel-studded throne,
to synagogue at Dura-Europos on Euphrates.
& tolerance of "dura"
A temple of Zeus Theos, a temple of Bel,
A mithraeum, a synagogue, a Christian baptistry
formal vocabulary same everywhere
and art like Greek Koine understand in all
craters of a new world, but world became hindered.
Your Blavatsky, her moves worked the phenomenon.

Dear Ghazal Mosadeq,

> The study origins for a wisdom childe
> studying her face for always in notice mode watching
> studying a face in motion
> on the chest of the amulet
> I am studying I am studying
> I am studying small brow
> the little groove a hieroglyph
> I am studying your Iran of mysteries
> I stare into your large eyes
> I am studying your appetite and resistance
> and tactile fringes so every mark in your poetry
> reasons to get what it needs, O Hafiz
> is reason a need?
> I promise
> I will study *your life* and for your life as long
> as I have life is what you saw to advise
> to know the dance turns the wheel
> turns the devilish inside the body coil, in Chefchaouen
> the Sufi women turn in the blue dawn in their feminist pride
> I have that tendency learning from you

Dear Eleni-mou,

> Zeus survived because of Serapis
> the cross, the fish, the anchor, the leering
> Jonah under the gourd a sleeping Endymion
> lamb carrier, our land as
> hieratic—the apse.
> Christians started burying their dead in sarcophagi
> fourth-century Tunisia manufactured terra-cotta bowls
> for burial, who mythologized Christian/Jewish subjects
> as two spheres of tolerance in the arts.
> burial chambers under St. Peter's, ancient mythology
> A unique *projecta* a bridal casket upon which a
> crucifix was next to the toilette of Aphrodite
> barbarian vivisection in the west and rise of Islam in the east
> Palmyrene Syria
> Arch of Constantine—renaissance critics like Ghiberti & Vasari
> a thorough disentangle of classical forms
> begging of dark ages to revive light!
> overcame by art of Italian Renaissance will make you beg, buy, and steal
> I am running on the syncretic wind now, forgive me
> I confess I am hungry for gnosis as you are, go to your Greeks!
> and I will be unfaithful to the degraded structures
> Help me, I am hungry, dear wise daughter of day and night
> I want to know

Dear Laurie,

　　"I Can't Stand the Rain,"
lost this, her memories, a gnosis
If we didn't have, rejects we wouldn't have much of us
Anohni—her song "I Fell in Love with a Dead Boy"
John Shaffer
NY shuffle
double reed of apricot wood
così for your glass and mine vocal four minutes
Akilah remembers Smyrna
remembers
papa—symbolic, "Eileen"
1919 NYC If you love them it's a dream
Fado "Young Man Blues" Mose Allison
nomads back into the night on the lonely Mongolian steppes
long your melancholy as much as ecstasy
Dvořák could master, we'll remember the NY shuffle
I am distorted, and always would lie and stall to hear
a fabulous song again

Dear Selah,

　　I like illusion
Too much of them that split
the dichotomy of chance in Art
how here now?
the marvelous burden of blue splits
she's a spy fixed in another room
the slits in my body leaking sorrow
mystery in the edges of protest, a ripped page
who are we? can we split in shoguns?
in their mouths, lip split, the splitting sound of shotguns
catch each other in our mouths
as we take a jewel for our University!
for the body—but don't court atrophy
It's so long ago after our teacher is dead
put away plaits, many centuries
and the anti-pagan discourse
of the missionaries developed
spilt blood.
silence.
our time now to take Buddhism back to China?
but not of faith but of endurance, empathy
no more no more but to *tha ma gyi shes pa*
I confess I am only a con-glomeration
a con-evangelist
Of tendencies, no god I serve

Dear Neighbor,

    boarded up now with all bluster & death
    12 Chairs where the Jewish waiter
    was not going to agree with the state
    more tyrants to spit upon
    naked Palestine, a split map, three cups
    sat down at the crossroads, a topography
    image of Jarnot on the screen of my dream
    on "parent"—as medicator,
    a wise mendicant
    a feud on death row
    out of entrapment to remember
    the guns in Beirut and how worlds turn
    as she took in one who was homeless
    what I didn't do

Dear Confessor,

    to get bashed and rounded up in orange plastic
    nets on Fifth Avenue, don't hurt my head, please oh mister cop man
    glass splitting
    Spitting Glass
    To watch is to remember the art flew past us
    not nostalgia, but continuum, so quickly
    I confess I could never catch up
    All our beauty
    all we do, did was twitch in our progressive "past"
    with lithe totem on my shrine continuum
    which says sleep with more friends to know the world,
    bodies go fast
    of growing up in them
    a voice & body, create a "fairy ring"
    you fill in the gaps for all the winged
    creatures a collage
    parting waves to escape turbulence?

Dear Ancestor,

    systems that don't work
    conjure adjustment
    not a free-for-all
    Petrarch's "thread of life which unto me was given"
    dumpster diving with planets
    edible trees, knots
    content, I feel you, "this soul Siren who with us doth dwell"
    not resolving where to set the lantern,
    the key, the icon, the story
    Want to stay playful
    But hate all the suffering in this
    depraved madhouse
    cruel brutal death-house
    The pathological Capitalocene
    masters of all war greed
    The trickery the lies the ignorance
    The foul money
    Feeling sick in complicity
    Disgust, where's love now?
    Poetry where *thy* sting & power?
    Liberation now, nothing enough
    Never did enough. Never did enough.

Dear Zoe,

    Angel Gabriel protecting a child's body
    St. Agnes & Ursula
    & all who command protection
    my matriarch & confessor be sacrificed as a
    hierophant,
    the winds of wild change &
    circumstance may we not be in
    a riot of this life as mental protesters
    studying mere images
    studying feet against a tide
    clothes with flowers
    the wrath of the torn and the mended messes
    & masses.
    resolve the pain, heal the wounded

Dear William S. Burroughs,

Do you want to tell of it? As then, so now.
again, a new drug
become the solution out of serotonin hell
would you assassinate to cure the messes the mind makes
strangle or—
a branch of the recent events
what I should to you turn down here, the heat
upheaval infection lurks
break that harm that love could do
tell me to do that and won't endeavor
to be a danger in the way

—————————————————————————————

Dear Future Poets,

tissues in letters
obviate
explode
don't swallow their words
dialectic moon & hideout, don't
vanish but keep calm
keep civil
keep head on
moon or Mars
who is the queerest wheel
keep hard plow
fill out new frontiers
can we extract from all dimensions
for poetry's pride
I have pride, forgive me
Again, please praise me
and then repeat after me
and praise yourself
"We are the guard!"

from Anne, who confesses her pride

Stave 6

An aria for the vibrant realms of wilderness playgrounds / strophes of passion, / transcending all maps global / worry states of mind. / Not kept us turning, parsing, samsara, a great egoic wheel / our little tribe in the yard on Halloween / and enunciation with a bouquet / keeps returning, out of gut invincible with habitual desire and "end border patrol" / Capitalocene the great adepts rise to end border patrol / We were pirates and handsome. / And developing more markets. / Okay to be architectural, an agora hides aggression but simplicity in fabulous junctions of citizens / say okay to the Greek alphabet. / To be effective I steeled up in the role of translator for the nomad commune and interpreted airplane jokes and all pods & telepathics to travel the trade routes to come back to mother ship on the out-lot with its spigots of poetry. / always poetry. but set up the mantra instead inside border patrol. / about needing caravanserai of mind to be a vessel & vassal and what the shepherd had endured nonetheless six realms were urns of evidence on a wheel, a hellish vortex of babble as they churned traces of Mesopotamia's mirage / looking to land we had memorized. / How to break the illusion of material barrier, free radicals, / but lying about what so-and-so had done to cast the first stone. / So to get there you had to be there and get the drift / shift the mind a tad upward. / Trade some hostages. / Behind antler-mind singing / as if we were coaxing what had obscured tangles of memory / we unlocked mystery / Cecilia Vicuña / picture her always and one more time we love her and we rage / because the hell was upon us savage and she mouthed it whispering / and we were trapped in the dust of a nuclear blast, ravaged / the desert held / It was already the '50s the transformation had started. / We sang together / Ambrose controlled my volume. / Cecilia walked through it.

"plaited lines that extend"

Extinction Aria, Its Exegesis, the Realms:
How Ink Is Blood

And this was my vision
rocked back by the
weirdness of days
days on earth when
the weather changed course
when we lost our minds
when leaders failed us
there was no wisdom
everyone was joking
everyone was very entertaining
when war kept going
and animals were mimicking the end
and starving kept on
and there were people escaping
across many borders
dying of it, the running
you bent to see them on the map
borders were lines on a map
you strained at the screen
little dots
people were dots on the map
points of light with beating hearts
they can see us anywhere
we said
we looked at ourselves
are these people?
(are we yet people?)

and people were trying to escape
and were weeping
and no one could speak
and these too,
are people are they people?
they could be cruel and hateful in speech
it was Babel time
bubbling up
it was all the end-time prophecies
coming into focus
they had been inked before our time
it was all in writing
it was a contract an oracle
no escape
they had been etched for extinction
the song, the exegesis, the realms
how ink is blood

but more like a prelude to end-times
obsessive
your mind can't get off
a jag
can't cut the dark dream
streaming in
missing advocate of praise:
imagination or divination

could not bear to feel joy
what was joy
on the other side of the world?
was prosperity joy?
was power
what was it
inside yourself
confounded interpretation
how can you be joy
and how be joy when
and if not joy, art
if on other side of the world
if on there that place—mind-stream of
dirt on ice, a forgotten place—
deep inside when you give up
how feel when on and loop this back
who can you want to be, people
I sing with damaru, *I sing with syllables*
E Ma Ho!

If days are quiet hell realms are raging
don't be fooled
hell might seem modest it conflates
it is entangled
uninterrupted hell, rage

hot and raging
and ink is blood
and ink is stain is serum is blot
and ink the bloodroot
& brooding of blood
and ink blueing
and ink running
and ink a blunder
and blush of ink will ride
and ink a body
and ink a nomad
and ink will hold a book
ink a bomb
but obsolete
and ink a mind
bold with neurons
inked bones
never buried
borders of ink
brazen ink
inked
instinct
inscribe
mark my word
mark my blood
stain of the poet
mineral embers
If they are sunny, hell realms
remember allegiance
to fire and to how fire
may burn and torture a victim
how can you just say this in ink
there's blowback
to the telling
self-immolating

fire is radiation
a twist of sickness
if one has murdered a body,
if one and one's minions
have scorched the body,
earth body,
if one has been unmindful
and this of anger and its flames
will reap destruction in
all directions of space and
you will hear song,
a sobbing song
hot and cold realms
sing everywhere when caught by fear
a fearing song, a rasp

If one is exceedingly
destructive of forests,
of citadels, of structures both ancient
modern too that go straight
up into the sky high,
higher than tallest tree
so high and where beings dwell
then we all suffer

say we are not so vertical
not so intervening as that
suffer fumes, suffer ash,
suffer unholy air
suffer on the plains,
on mountaintops we escape to
or if inattentive to the way
flames lick the mountain,
where oil fields may be set smoking,
then hot hells will have minion

they will melt the mind
and all good intention
corrupt artifice of your plan
for the exegesis of realms
skull will turn dust
other creatures will suffer as fire consumes
more phenomenal worlds
all you put in fire's way
when aggression lashes out,
no roads are safe
and children hide under leaves
having nightmares
about being "droned" down
set aflame, perpetual anxiety
hot hells coming easily to warmongers
coming easily into the slippery dark age,
come with hot hell weaponry
even the *dakinis* weep

Ink resolves itself
and it cools
and it is residue for the lonely
and cold calculation, a cyber war
tell it to the ink
ink is your last chance
ink is amorphous
it might recede from view
it returns
maybe you vanish off the canvas
you are still (dead) life
cools hearts drop way below
zero, frosty, turned like a blade
a shoulder against you

If they are icy, they are the dagger,
they are in stasis, frozen
edge of a diamond crystal
if the cold hells are unresponsive
it is because they resist language
they have no way to measure poetry
no way to think of poetry, it slips away
and only crystalline minds will hear
locked up in a vault of resistance
they are a zipper,
they are airtight container,
they are solid
if they are dangerous it is because
they are nascent they are spectral
you see your image frozen
in time hands so brittle
they break
and walking, no where to go
sing again: no where to go
frozen in attitude,
holding tight position,
freeze before they relent
if the birds are weak and can't fly
butterflies won't land
if you never feel empathy
you are in a cold hell,
lips sealed no song escapes
and arms won't provide embrace
a monument of stone
and if stone could freeze
it would crack and shatter
into particles of ice
shards that sting and wound
cut and will draw blood
mind is in perpetual lockdown set against itself

and trapped inside an ice palace
that as it melts
grows more strange,
why have you been hiding
your cold heart?
what endurance
if you crack the ice queen apart
you will see her brittle pearls,
brittle diamonds that gleam
and magnetize
it is a woman exploring genders and becoming
planets
identity you can watch
her morph and turn
her own wheel

Ink is your vehicle
and it will save
and it will sing
and it will make claim
and it will compel
and it will be a quest
and a humble object
and ink the intransient
hell would be fulfilled
when ink fails
you will hunger for it to drink it
ink is blood

If you are always hungry
needing wanting begging
you might waste away
the neck thins without substance
and the belly thickens
misfortune, misfortune

distraction for the hungry ghost
starving: you never get enough
little neck, poor bird
starving, so very hungry,
poor ghost
you hallucinate your desire
and it grows
labyrinthian
ever satiated, never fulfilled,
ghost of herself
if the mind is greedy,
if it desires and desires
it will be the bloated corpse
it will find all treasure turn to ache
in the belly
the fix is in, the fix is in
o hungry ghost!
all nourishment turn poison
so very hungry
a crust of bread, poor ghost
desire desire
and thwarted
beams of light trying to reach you
thought mechanisms churn
the hungry ghost demons
too weak to be brought to anger

preta, preta, preta
eat me alive
dance till you go mad
drinking blood
ghost on the job
no rest
grasping
preta preta

And ink is witness
and ink makes you turn inside
you are writing this on your hands
you are always writing
in invisible ink
etched on mind's screen
animal mind
my restlessness
want your mind to sprout wings
grow fins, horns
want your mind
to be my sweet tame animal
ho!
sex at ready
ready to pounce
ready to mount
animal
lore of the animal
animal that will never rest
trembling in ink blood
phantasmagoria animalia
chaos & cosmos
become throat of the lynx

If the animal is at rest it is secretly leaping
in a dream, REM sleep, waiting
to ambush
it is a big cat it is the tiger you mount
you carry your banner to the wind
E Ma Ho, E Ma Ho!
when the animal is remembering
it is back 60 million years
it is swimming and then
it will come to land
to breathe the air of land

it will morph and retain memory
it will breathe air
even the wolf will ease its body
to sniff at air
and return to lair

And ink traces this gesture
a kind of self-possession
imposes itself on the animal
willing to be a fool
willing to stalk
willing to pounce and kill
willing to survive
ink is its master
ink talks and survives
ink tames the unruly
get into the dense shadow
of your animal vulnerability
puts a trace to itself, ink
the whale remembers, etched in time
all the birds scored for enumeration
all beauties of the heart
and of the angel fish
there will be luminous color now
there will be light
the owl will hoot back at you
and night all inky descend
genres in a kind of hierarchy
up the ladder
If the human is lying down it is pretending
it is an "it" it is a she, it is a not-she,
it is a we a they
it pretends and does not know
what it is
it thinks I am this, the human is under the influence

of humanness, of becoming human
it troubles
it waxes
it is atavistic
it does not want to wander anymore
can't stop
cybernetic capacity
a dance
but destroys as it wanders
it communicates
it is the best at this
in all the realms
it can talk
take risk
that's what it means to be human
and language is its ink
is imperiled
not-he, but something in between is desirous
human wants to be between
it is complex
O human
the contour of you is innocent
but because you make up things
you are dangerous
ever in incantation
you are aggregate
porous, ahistorical
don't get it, don't get it
ridding the world of all but you
humble objects
where are they
everywhere in the landscape
you notice?
go be looking
that tree which is an ash

sit down under
the walking trees

And want to have legs in ink
and want to be my own portrait
a full portrait
ink will tell it all
light & shade
nuance of the hidden
a bee in the ear of the human
the starling in the beak of the human
how talk to the wind
and come to god
If the warmonger is inventing a battle cry
he, always he, is readying to go
and he thinks
I am a god
you will know this by an easy slogan
words will be cheap
I am a g-g-g-god
its simple words that are signaling assemblages
that have power
if the warmonger is insistent
he is surprising himself—him it is always him—
he is then turning to the mirror of himself
to worship himself
and then turning if he seems to trace an enemy
he needs to do this, he will
it is what he is doing
an imprint for the psyche
for the habit
this is the apparatus of becoming
enemy is the creation of a warring god realm
of becoming embattled
isolated

and a kind of ghostly corporeality
the white ghost
the slaver
hunter of indigenous ones
knows no solitude, the karmic nightmare
scaffolding doom
bought nature inside
and ripped its guts no umbrage
the warrior a sum total
but with *dorje* & *phurba*
brandishing power
da da da da da ta ta
late in capital
late interiors
what happened to the vast landscape outside
fold the metaphor for your sensation
filtered out of memory
love?
what was it
only after a kill
could you love?
your own death
experience of passing through
there is no enemy but the one manufactured
a beautiful enemy worthier than you are
holds secret of poetry
da da da da da ta ta!

ink knows this
in creating weaponry
lights the optic nerve
look long and hard
you will be a machine of death
the drawings are complex
they fly they go up in the sky
you can be a child, again

and as you die you see red
ink knows the creation of enemy
ink would be harmonious in duty
would be harmless blind unseen were
it not enemy calling ink to task
in telling in becoming
if it weren't for enemy
flailing its wares
ever-new economies of things to
go tonally gray
the marks respond to an inner clock
wind down and explode
a grid
a grip
spirals lop and waves ink make
when it is blood
it is vertigo
it is a kind of revelation
the enemy was recognized by
his uniform, hair standing on end
the terra-cotta warrior inside the mind
the pink of rocks becoming pink of sky
as you die
selling weapons you love to make
to the enemy
ink settles here like the blood it is
ink making a kind of ancestry, a mark
rapid deployment
swift calculation
though you sit thousands of miles away
consult your chart of doom
ink as negative space winding around itself
the coil the web of entrapment
alternative realism
conviction the ink says
it says right here we must win

ink is the challenge
ink a drawing as embodiment of idea
last call before you amass wealth
ink as a method to see our concept of the world
a world of undulation
like the sea creatures remember when they are in sea
and stroked as they drown

deva, deva loka
place of the gods
anything you want
all the pleasures you could ever imagine
and they are hoarded
jewels cluster around the neck
oceanic ripples of all exorcisms
thrill the chakras
drugs are nothing compared
to the ecstasy of the god realm
will you age?
will the seat get hot and
you fall off

*the sky is not blue
and will not hold*

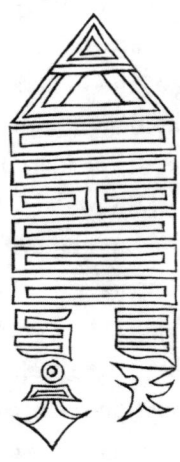

Extinction Dirge

Luxury condos / offshore oil
is that what
the creeps say who murder children in their sleep
is that what the cushy ones say?
moonlight was not coming forth in this genocide
sunlight was not coming forth in this genocide
listen, the soothsayer said, for the dangerous ground
is bathed in blood that curdles the cradle
the blood comes forth the blood speaking
the blood gushing the blood screaming
comes forth in the genocide

Stave 7

Accounting in the semblance of time / meet the other mouth with a different tongue / A countdown on the precipice / old and young. / Frames of fractal movement. / Edits & disruptions of this text, you all help mess. / Fleshy mess. / Mixing it up to sort the mess/distress, the illusion/intrusion. / Will you all please help my Armistice? / We all met years ago reading *Nomadology: The War Machine* / As the migrant leaves everything behind, the nomad does not depart. / And a nomad may wear jewels as weapons, shiny, pointed / But also naked nomad, unbuffed. blunt. burnt. / entrapped. / The migrant clings to space left by the receding forest / I never slept the same way since. / I remember the first class in the Free School with the scholarly philosophers talking about vision & trance / they were noncommittal / I could see end-time in the settlements. / I counted for a year, see this. / I was coming to, but we were losing our building, our clubhouse / poetry-sound-text-base / And hauling buckets of water from the yard. / Becoming migrant.

an Aramaic term: BETH NAHRAIN
"my house of two rivers"
Tigris-Sumer Idigna
from Old Persian:
Ufratu—*hui perthuua*
meaning "good to cross over"
tigra meaning "rapid"
Apkallu: "half man/half fish"
Shiny carps of the sea at the time of the Flood
A flood sent by the god, to wipe out humankind
Humankind was too noisy, we said, at the time of the Flood.

"like a bronze chain into eternity."

The Counting: Echolocation

Part 1:

We met pink,
the earth turned blue.

1. we met in Saqqara
2. the earth turned
3. blue then crimson
4. I blew the blue
5. in a generation of making that's what they'll say about us
6. they killed the earth, they killed each other
7. street urchin
8. a long robe, they killed language!
9. in solitude, you said "maroon"?
10. like a nun . . .
11. I blew the blue
12. the earth turned blue
13. And in solidarity
14. for children, against AR15s
15. Labor Strike March
16. eviscerated cities
17. red white blue
18. I blew off the blue
19. "I basically stalked you," you said
20. "during the housing crisis"
21. it was "say hello to A for me"
22. that kind of day
23. the echo of snippets
24. It's never an accident, overheard
25. prophets before exile: Nahum, Zephaniah, Jeremiah
26. after exile: Moloch, Obadiah
27. listen to your prophets
28. their "astral omens"

29. "auspicious coincidence" (tendrel)
30. how to convene
31. take this coincidence for art-in-life
32. all the prophets' eyes
33. what the eyes say when you meet
34. Ezekiel 6 evictions of the "natives" who bring the *ʒahir* to humanity
35. the path
36. a path of tendencies
37. and it will sing and manifest
38. Miriam, Deborah, & Huldah joining
39. And I said I was alone because radical poets were lazy that day
40. And I was heading to the depths of the deepest dark forest
41. But everyone around us screaming
42. they kill one another
43. and we were more silent in our mission
44. they kill poetry
45. Fifth Avenue, to lure them out into protest
46. parting the Red Sea
47. "Endurance" was the Buddhist acronym for our planet
48. not White Extinction Anxiety
49. not what she wanted   remember
50. the Masters of War
51. her eye is storm-wind,   must endure
52. photosyntopia
53. and her mouth is
54. strengthened
55. by the energy of plants
56. and potential
57. most agricultural
58. civilizations
59. is more
60. and potential of most of wisdoms
61. for women,
62. no safe border crossings

63. implicit, implode. We talked about our generation, the guys. He had it. A few others. Sam Shepard presented new ways of thinking in theater and in language who seemed to ride in deep core making with refreshed energy like winged horse, like an arrow. There's Tibetan word: *lungta* which translates "wind horse." Uplifted force . . . it rides into you, you ride it, its ethos, mind-state, and implies an act of meeting whatever life has dished up with spontaneity, sharpness, & worth.

64. remember Sam, his life around glorious horses.

65. stamina crossing secure borders

66. of not what he is but she & they

67. is in power

68. we had power, 1960s

69. *(wanted) Utopian, not fright of the world*

70. A play on your heart, in language

71. & standards

72. hunting-and-gathering

73. a quieter mode of shelter

74. she wants Hesiod

75. she wants Homer: the proud Hippomolgoi, drinkers of milk,

76. and the Abioi, most righteous of all men

77. O hunting

78. and we gather mimosas

79. sporadic trances

80. remember the stage, remember the danger

81. run by ominous, not cradling men

82. and with humble obedience owed to

83. this male authority.

84. O, perform!

85. cradle to page

86. not dust

87. or discord

88. and we gather

89. preferring the garments with pine oil

90. a husband's
91. family. Greater latitude?
92. quaking the land
93. Seize our property, no, no, O come Hammurabic
94. and we gather
95. but we'll gather greater latitude after Herodotus visits
96. and the peacock spends the day keeping watch
97. Early Sumerians want to prosper and make war
98. but the world has been turned upside down
99. come back to the oracular chamber
100. greater latitude of women, the bull's whip
101. telling many things that would happen in the future
102. not what Mara demanded
103. a fettered cage
104. and gathered
105. out of Florida a synthesis of escape
106. Ha, religion. early
107. power to female sexuality and
108. early law gave
109. women property but also listening
110. to inner voice twixt action and sleep
111. not outright
112. property
113. the glistening lapis lazuli scepter
114. but cultic importance waxes and wanes
115. entering the land of enchantment
116. as in daylight
117. home of the bomb
118. a mind of Babylon
119. could you be the lyre of another?
120. men and women go out before you as a single thread
121. it stands out, mind
122. and dangle before you
123. that tree, that is mine
124. in a soul of evolution

125. you see
126. they killed him once they killed him twice
127. here, they killed him like an Antichrist
128. we study Achille Mbembe
129. and learn the charnel ground
130. how certain Sumerian theatricals built on a battleground
131. for understanding the Celtic god of fire
132. magic tricks the sun
133. burns to death on
134. "its ontological limit"
135. roaring or ruining land
136. a double standard
137. for the great city returning
138. law and you will notice blanks in chronology
139. a reticular world
140. after
141. Sumerian times
142. a fear of snakes
143. woman's virginity
144. on
145. marriage block
146. locked up in necrotic cells
147. a veil on the excavations
148. closing the epic
149. the veil over the ziggurat
150. poet's role in community
151. "respectable" vesanic times
152. filled in
153. in public to emphasize
154. modesty.
155. hiding the devil in the details
156. the veil, the villain
157. the valley
158. Emblature.
159. filled in

160. Hamm and Urabic code
161. your presence in the reeds
162. given over   the veil
163. a serious matter
164. prescriptions
165. cures & punishments
166. assuring
167. protections but clearly
168. echoes of protection
169. limits &
170. inferiority.
171. no staves
172. O
173. civilization
174. women,
175. upper
176. more credit
177. filters like dreams
178. powerful queens.
179. Sibyl of Cumae
180. beautiful you know her
181. and the bough-tree
182. and gather her
183. as doors fly open
184. Nefertiti,
185. less discord in the land
186. avaunt the viper moon
187. Akhenaten
188. disputes in this reign.
189. gather by River Lethe
190. 2400 BC
191. Mesopotamian Omens
192. that an Egyptian writes,
193. inside the mind of another person
194. Ptahhotep, writes toward

195. the Babel story morphing to Ziggurat
196. anyone in the early civilizations:
197. and knowing this
198. O, make the sound, men; try emphasis
199. and we laugh in our many tongues
200. as toils for our times, stop fighting
201. "If you are a man of note, found for
202. yourself a household, fill it with poetry
203. and love your wife at home and anywhere, as it beseems.
204. Fill her with freedoms
205. belly, clothe her back . . ."
206. dream of her, let go
207. have her back, really have it
208. but stave off!
209. the mastery.
210. inspired awe like the sea
211. Remember
212. the abzu like an oar
213. her eye is her storm-wind,
214. remember the visit to Nippur
215. and her v——— & mouth are
216. strength you'll never know
217. archetypes are mere *mutaformas*
218. like philosophers, saints
219. Simone Weil
220. M. L. King
221. on property, law
222. Martha Graham, in costume
223. be sure who the heirs were—
224. erratic humans in this quest
225. remember
226. the vertical scaffold to the stars
227. the storm-
228. the erratic rhizome
229. wind

230. wind
231. that is her language
232. eye everywhere media-res
233. wind
234. and storming
235. disassembling
236. remember performing
237. puncturers in the human
238. ornamental, form
239. prosperity in the lovers
240. their drag
241. why?
242. (pause)
243. and in Chinese and may have
244. also in India and,
245. (pause)
246. Been storm-wind
247. Dream of Dumuzi
248. later, in Western Europe.
249. keeping it safe
250. Patriarchalism, in sum, a dance
251. a threshold
252. umbilicus
253. and deepen how deepen
254. what was the whispered sentence?
255. the urge toward disharmony
256. religious
257. woman
258. behind walls
259. you
260. not revolt
261. form networks
262. and escape the drones
263. seaferns
264. older

265. shifting illusion of democracy
266. a bacterial cell controlled by a chemically synthesized genome
267. and many daughters-in-law
268. as well as out-of-law daughters,
269. shape
270. of love
271. enforcing
272. patriarchalism,
273. family
274. echoing
275. assumptions
276. false patterns
277. of patriarchy
278. dictated female infants killed
279. mercilessly
280. in throes of
281. population
282. control.
283. oh
284. and murder coming for the enemy line
285. murder most foul the killing
286. of a glamourous prince
287. mixtures of advantages & disadvantages it is
288. still Narcissus
289. body always harmed and the polis
290. the plot of
291. never like Etruscan times?
292. never so attenuated
293. early
294. civilization,
295. wet light in the eyes
296. early body Kennedy, a spree of
297. bootlegging
298. and late
299. gaelic glee

300. how far a body?
301. how far a body to travel?
302. and stretch more than 2,000 years,
303. that would long shape
304. a long shape, body
305. barracudas
306. a longing shape
307. what happened, murder most foul
308. echoing
309. Middle East, and fury
310. northern Africa, and southern Europe.
311. Separate
312. and arise, along
313. Tigris-Euphrates
314. a mirror of memory
315. how THE WHOLE EARTH had one language
316. and the same words
317. my covenant
318. a dizziness of freedom
319. my further crescent
320. my father crescent
321. future brow,
322. ziggurat to Marduk
323. poet cutting edges
324. of static
325. Civilization,
326. as a complex,
327. apocalypse
328. vibrant crescent
329. open mic on the Senate floor
330. disputed and
331. disputatious, grievous
332. assassination
333. shape of a crescent
334. a neon hymen

335. my brown heart, a fingernail
336. culling and grasping
337. planning a trip to Jupiter's
338. moon Europa
339. an ocean of liquid water
340. part of the world. a lift of off world water
341. beneath an icy shell
342. $5.2 billion NASA mission
343. more satellites in space
344. gnats, birds, ghosts
345. it is important to ask more
346. of blueprint of cosmos
347. and harvest songs
348. what traces
349. TV episodes
350. what faces, traces
351. a true detective
352. of river-valley of folk song
353. remember rural light
354. rural texture
355. Plot apparatus:
356. to have characters
357. an idea of ballad,
358. a clear melody floating
359. idea of assassination and revenge
360. people and shadows
361. people creating new histories
362. calendars with high holy days
363. look up
364. idea of ceremony
365. builders' heads
366. a coda, cracked by the fall of scaffolding

(everything adventuring after a civil war)

Part 2: codes mean:

irrigation, earth interrupted, fragments
iron use, more productive grain seeds,
the potter's wheel, a bard wheel
        Money & idea of writing codices
        did the use of
        certain medicinal drugs, help plot law?
        Attribute and of foreign codices, enemies of archive
        consequences for Bruegel. Our Herminuisance, a strategy, the
        dancing elfins

wheels of river-valley
        never had to be redone.
        Her brow, another codex, another fragment
        crossed in this crescent, a Dylan song
        cultures, a
        race, a rasp in the shadow, idiot wind
        I'll love and conquer to tell our Time
        flood story and mafia momentum
        words that chime with "cartel"
        such as the
        Sumerian-derived
        "alcohol"—
        such that
        and other
        transmissions.
        petty murderers, political "spooks"
        Instruments to work the diagnostic
        our life in clinamen
        (harps, drums,
        flutes) diagetic
        seven-orchestral and eight-tone trance
        scales now are ready

and towers and now
columns now common
and now common
and now common in Muslim and in European
and in American architecture
How is it a note
of your song?
sleepwalking

based the ziggurats
perhaps and columns
continuities in edginess
ideas of divine kingship, angles of sunlight
Coba, *bab-ilim*. gate of god
and then and now worked out
in later Roman, an idea
to step aside?
have influenced the beautiful dreamer
in ethereal democracy
have later
African monarchies.
stepped out?
Influence was it stepped up?
Con-
fluence
and have empire
and empirical
humanity
as part of a larger natural
harmony, not a steppe's profit
not abandoned Mesopotamia
held humans separate from nature, capable

but capricious in terror?

nature
as antagonistic
mistake not seeking in peace a price of generosity
and in it delve, devour
within it. your rage.

action & anxiety,

not fear
greater tranquility
as India; some of these

the Sumerian worldview.
women closer to nature
in an archive of eco-feminism

transmitted it
cultures
Greek,
Christian, and the scare quote
Muslim. Who you admire most
Most "modern religion":
a leap of mind
would send out different signals,
invasions intercepts
getting the mastery, Allah
then a craving for the ziggurat again
she asked that these be included in revamp

that it be a city and with the graces of
the cosmos and the grace of the multiverse
and that eyes would be in all pores of the
stars: Mesopotopia, our edgy angular
shape-shifting bodies, pocked
and first of all care for these world bodies
refracting from the intelligence of astral ones
what shape is the true cradle? Cascade?
who will take care of?
Mesopotopia we said *our city*
      the mess we made of it
swerve of holding in motion, in arrears
that something would have to be held and slide a fort in
      cling -amen
that it could not go empty
          cling-a-man
like a nest
they like to say empty nest / flees the child, clinamen
What is Indra? saw a saint meditating, a whole rishi whose
body turned diamond after the body decayed
Carried a weapon, a weapon of cradle or of boomerang
Hold forth my drug
You cannot bribe for your ego trip
Samaya is a command out of nowhere
Where arise?
I, the cradle

Part 3:

The girl-girt-belt binds to the grave *in confusio linguarum*
Hinge that cuts air, mother-belt instrumentalizes
A right person uses the cradle . . . who?
Destroys like . . . who? what? a diamond bullet
Strikes dealing accuracy once it loses

having destroyed, comes back
To your own hand. Fingerprints point to your own hand
Wading in a theme of cradling civilization that it would
Come round to haunt you, O woman
you wrote this to quell this
fear of what you did not know about the two rivers
Waters of life
Does it help visualize off the cadaver you study
In conspiracy
I have a map to show you of my heart, my trans heart
how poison is medicine but how I loved you
in evolution how I loved *my* world
I had no back
and no one had my back
the monkey grinder in the dream
was the Scythian Gustave Moreau
a mystical windup doll, up I went on empty, *poupée* the factotum
and I said to myself: your poem flows to magnify the data files
Dear Anne: you wrote, because you asked of these things:

THE GEOPOLITICAL CENTER OF THE WORLD'S

FRAGMENTATION IS

PRECISELY THE PLACE WHERE UNIFICATION BEGAN

UNDER THE NAME CIVILIZATION

5,000 YEARS AGO . . .

IF A CERTAIN GEOPOLITICAL CHAOS SEEMS TO BE

TAKING HOLD OF THE WORLD IT'S IN

IRAN IRAQ &

SYRIA, RUSSIA & CHINA AND THIS IS DRAMATICALLY

DEMONSTRATED IN THE EXACT

LOCATION WHERE

CIVILIZATION'S GENERAL SETTING IN ORDER BEGAN.

WRITING, ACCOUNTING, ROYAL JUSTICE,

PARLIAMENT, INTEGRATED FARMING &

OTHER & LIFE A SCIENCE, MEASUREMENT, POLITICS,

RELIGION

POPULACE INTRIGUE AND PASTORAL POWER

WAY OF GOVERNING "FOR THE GOOD OF THE

SUBJECTS" FOR THE SAKE OF THE FLOCK

AND ITS WELL-BEING—EVERYTHING LUMPED INTO

WHAT WE STILL CALLED

CIVILIZATION—WAS ALREADY 3,000 YEARS AGO

BEFORE JESUS CHRIST

WAS THE MARK OF THE KINGDOMS OF AKKAD &

SUMER.

A NEW IRAQI STATE?

STATE-DIRECTED HUMANITY IS DEAD.

THE GHOST OF THE DEAD WON'T BE SUBDUED BY TNT

COMPARED TO TRANSNATIONAL; [POWERS THE

STATES CAN NO LONGER MAINTAIN

THEMSELVES EXCEPT IN THE FORM OF HOLOGRAM]

THE GREEK STATE IS NO LONGER ANYTHING MORE

THAN A CONVEYOR OF

INSTRUCTIONS IT HAS NO SAY IN.

THE BRITISH STATE WALKS TIGHTROPE WITH BREXIT

CONTINUOUS AVALANCHES OF SCANDAL IN ITALY,

SPAIN, BRAZIL . . .

PRESENT-DAY CAPITALIST STATES ARE ENGAGING IN

AN EXERCISE

OF METHODICAL SELF-DISMANTLING . . .

SEPARATIST TEMPTATIONS ABOUND. A FORM OF

UNENDING CIVIL WAR . . .

FACADES REMAIN BUT MASK THE RUBBLE . . .

WE ARE IN A PRODIGIOUS REVERSAL OF THE PROCESS OF

CIVILIZATION

THE MORE IT INSPIRES TO UNIVERSAL COMPLETION, IT

IMPLODES AS A FOUNDATION—

THE MORE THE WORLD AIMS FOR UNIFICATION, THE

MORE IT FRAGMENTS

THE CAUSE OF THE ATMOSPHERE AND THE PLANET

OFFERED CIVILIZATION

THE IDEAL PRETEXT FOR ITS COMPLETION

THE PRESIDING AUTHORITIES WERE WITHIN AN INCH OF

DECLARING THE UNIVERSAL

AND ECOLOGICAL IMPERIUM MUNDI

IN THE "INTEREST OF US ALL"

THE MAJORITY OF THE HUMAN AND NATURAL MILIEUS,

CUSTOMS,

& FORMS OF LIFE, THE TELLURIC CHARACTER OF EVERY

EXISTENCE

ALL THAT WOULD HAVE TO YIELD BEFORE THE

NECESSITY OF UNITING A HUMAN

SPECIES

WAS RENDING, WAS READING, WAS HEARTRENDING

Nothing happened at Copenhagen . . .
Lobby everyone for themselves
    Dismantling of all political unity

What's left of unity
but nostalgia for our central committee
to come together in front of the screens?

    One hears powerlessness
    finishing existence in the citadel
    Everyone is fleeing . . . this
    Playing the role of absent subscribers
    Packed up and left
    In fight, is inner or immobilized, a sinner
    Already elsewhere
    drug squad
    biggest hash dealer in France
    Life a marble
    Life a "god is dead" metabolism
    Life reserve
    Zarathustra
    More than Zarathustra
    Market capital
    Complications of Confucius
    Take warning: punishments for poets
    Modern sages don't push philology or tweak enough
    Let us out out out Mother Russia and her unrelated gods

The modernist literatures again
What the world needs now is beyond pictures
and is the youngers. who went through the commons and the
entheogens
Forbidden stuff of biome, the beautiful grace of Chinese
poetry
Not apocryphal but that they might still keep memory

I, the cradle
I, the candle
I, the ur-civilization
I, catastrophe of love

And You Shall Be Broken in Pieces

remnants of the land

[Isaiah 7:18] And it still shall come to pass
in that day
and it shall come that day in passing
and strange, unexpected, never told like this
with arrows with bows our passing
and it shall come and hither, in pieces they sang
because all the land shall become of hither born for a song
briars & thorns & targets
and you will be there, a blunt axe aiming
associate yourselves, but a weakened people
and ye shall be broken in pieces,
and give ear, all ye, of yore, ear of yourselves
blunt people, a blunt axe aiming and ear gone out like an eye
guard yourselves, elders
of all countries, with your weak tones
they never perceive you prophets
they percolate your mind to taunt, steal your words
guard yourself your orb broken in pieces
stumble and fall, and be broken in pieces
and be taken, remnant of heartier land, now wasted
who broke you? my beloved elders
as noon fades, unmoored you cannot hold the candle
the camera broken in pieces the mirror gone
faces of elders under glow, broken, can read no more
words go halting
Shulamite's words:
my abolition is spirit
new abolitionist spit
name is as ointment
poured forth

our bed is green
Shulamite, of crepe skin
Shulamite, the scream
as in dark cellular music,
your light gone out in war death
but my beloved is to me
as a cluster of campfire
old in suffering, we grow in it
the ashes the cinders broken in pieces
in the vineyard of mortality, camphor
how do they take care of us broken
my dove, that art in
the clefts of the rock is not your hidden place anymore
they chase you out, elders of the softer places
look from the mountains
of the leopards
look to their sleek destruction
[Isaiah 8:22] And they shall look unto the earth, truth & darkness,
dimness of anguish; and they shall be driven to darkness
where?
other places in the crevice?
and look onto earth
and behold trouble [truth] & darkness
& dimness if light will anguish the elders
be driven to darkness, o applicants, o supplicants
o elders
and they shall look into the earth, for a few handouts in this trouble
see dimness of fading anguish of the old & poor,
then returning the stone to its cradle, and who listened
a few handouts,
and they shall be driven mad
and what about us here later
our lines of lyric beauty for the elders? spare a few
lines, a few coins
empower our elders

spare a few lines a few coins for the elders
that they be fed and
a bed for the elders
their skin that moves
like lizards
and what about loquacity for elders?
why are they always misshapen?
always timid, elders?
where your expression would be empathy for elders
it breaks them
and your roots are reflected
on shimmers of living and the old world systems
ancient systems ancient Sumerians
and their scented herbs
cypress & myrrh, and living animals
and it shall come to pass in that day
the myths of illusion will die quickly, die hard
we will all see clearly suffering of elders
and how to absorb what you love what you still remember
what you can write and see as you float by
i want to take all the daily moments
coming to pass in that day
and turn it into this poem
why are you so cruel against the elders
and it shall come to pass
after long life
after radical life
after harnessing what is your truth
will you remember the elders?
after all the blessings to us, to notice and remember
there is a curve
of beautiful chart line of life missing
rings   hooves   quarry
many circles like a notebook missing there is a curve

there can be trembling because it is missed around the curve
hurdles to find the journey of life, the quantum leap of spine
we beg for your transparency & pleasure, your speech as elders
wealth of knowledge, sweat, time, laboriousness
there is restitution if we can speak
there is a way we explore ourselves, through the mashes "old man"
the way we collaborate on comfort in the body
on the deep fire, auto-de-fé
the mashed old man
on the quality of confidence
summon an old tongue to speak
take charge, and the women too and all who pass as human, elder
and it shall come to pass in that day that we could come in passing
and that we grow kinder
writing from "I":
identity
afterward
evolving
and it shall pass and coming that day won't be put together again if
passing and let it pass forgetting elders
the wisp of memory of elder
how she rocked me, elder
how she rocked us
keep showing up in the same way all the trance dance to get to be old
and turning
come out from hiding old ones, speak the word and turn
a kind of narration, hiding
don't fall under
although a fire of anger can be useful
as a flame of inspiration
come out
from the shady garden,
minstrels with harps & flutes & flageolet
citterns, kettledrums

inspire the jongleurs
Mester de Juglaría
come you scops
expand
all the essentials, and make them be heard from your ancient larynx
eyes, ears, nose, teeth, broken eyeglasses of the elders
the holy crown existed, the holy tiara existed not . . .
memory take me with you
an angle, the voice, mend
like that favorite
nautilus shell of citizen: skin & bone
the war in a name will it ever wash away, will the old be sheltered as
    their crisis never washes away
brain gone
for this body, open beyond on the war ground will it ever wash away?
left-sided circuitry, wound wound wounded
will it be washed
lineage of ownership will it slip away
writerly alderman, citizen
brash and graceful, skin & bones of elders
siege of a fascist enterprise
argonauts and elders
lutherans who know no humor
slow burn as you wash and dry the elders
in your composition of the song for the elders
palinode when i take the bard living inside me
and dash tongue out, lash tongue out
i am just light, fragile light snow
how i see color in the deep ocean darkness like fish that have
never known sunshine
i am your worst fear
    i am a stranger in this charnel ground
    but resolute

*i am surely in trouble, all my days, for these are the days my friends,
these are surely the days, the days, the days grow older my friends my friends*

Recital in Walking: Telepathy

for a new equinox

And the next day, someone in our cell arrested
I started to walk out in the lunar zone
Where we needed to be
Smoke, the reticulate gasp of strangulation
Air's avenger was gallery
This prison boy. Girl. Person. Elder.
Person in a fix, then would be liberated body?
The child looked at the painted gold gloves at dawn
earthly or heavenly?
we were three then
and related in poetry, riding in a hired car
and said many tricks
words to be used to be
anytime back through the mirror
but he had lingered behind
and Erika decided to become a lawyer
the carceral work with carceral life
she stood at the door in Denver and
noted every arrest and became a "paddy wagon" of resistance
Dualitude . . . in mountains, wiser
I ply the skin, "my trade," the human, she said, a summit
That trembles as flesh does, matrix
What do you see in all the pores
Scars of the human, breathing
An outer crust to set the dressers going
And he came to be a poet, as she mounted the
Hall of Justice
Or ever-finite energy, this is in a small
refuge where we watch the sky and flee as must

looking for X hiding in neighbor's closet
Hierarchy subordination, evidence at trial
And witness attrition, urgent
I had been hard and brutal as meaning took endurance
metabolism of the hummingbird
and one sang of Uttar's freedom and Ishtar's beauty
freedom of cis woman not ignoring itself
I started to walk out in the suburban refuge
"a drama in heaven proceeding our cosmos" was how we put it
ligature, harken, cherubic dignitaries who are ever as bird messengers
the birds who twitch and dive
Steeped outside in a battle with magical thinking
omnibus for code & list & formula
Accoutrements for the last vesper sip of elixir from Harappa
And make plans for future communes, coalitions of commerce, under the wire
Did someone fly into the Orient
Avicenna, did he as Ibn Sina speak our future?
Philosophy was a later problem.
I wouldn't stop reading to converse right now
Only the spear that made the wound would close it
What is your votive chemical operation as you enlist? I asked
as you flagged the bus out of the Blue Mosque and we parted
Sap of vapor moisture of planet, and dryness, the alarms of wealth.
In a new slang and there were snags like "roosters in your posture dead one,
a bed down of Jurassic, stay put" and so on
The scales are weighing as we sit and speak, it's a long session
Her body is not rational to him and he doesn't even know
now how to bury her, is a subtext
A mythical order in the Avestis Mound, I, the invented form "Saena
    Meregha"
Heroes & gents where you can stay inside: don't go out now, tender children
it's getting too hot, wait till you trust the voices
Back there is irrational, there is an albatross warning
Bodies scattered in the doomsday prophecy

Solomon says he understood the language of the birds
The last karst of places
Some held the royal sanctuary, some the people
Birds of the Recital rise in their struggle
Another kind of ornithology with only what has gone missing
The Aviary is empty tonight, I'll sing myself alone to bed, everyone
else camping on the front range on an Earth Day retreat
What would you choose for your disaster as you count steel
The 40 "hot articles" that are inhaled and lodged in lung tissue from
residual plutonium in the soil? You want that?
And these plutonium dioxide particles will release
their alpha decay energy producing internal doses of radioactivity?
Please pass that message on not to hide from
the ever-ignorant populace as you remake your power quote. Really?
How ranking the clasp of wrath
when it is singing trying to stir your form from inaction
The joy in the recognition of serf woe is that it? Others do bidding
More of meetings more recitals, more warnings, more notes,
assassinations, meditations, actions, memorials
Let's question the smirk, the deserter, the omen, the double agent
The birds, departure, celestial ascent and I had dreamed new again
Or fly out to sea, seek urgent desire, knowledge
Of Sea, where hide next under a calcified Mayan temple
where scholars study codices and write their own jungle songs
Thinking how the birds suffer fires
Let's stretch the episode to wings over water, o seabirds
their names tell stories even if they fly far away
and I lived before
66 million years in a winged mode
Something will complete the circle of the birds
New-made life-form
They set out in thousands
Mimicries and artificial wings
Rotation of obligation

Year after year traveling
Crossing mountains of relay stations
Whole robotic bird elves spent on the journey
Drones of sorrow for the PTSD controllers
Many disappear after they complete construction
destruction
Drowned with the detritus
Some burnt to ashes by the heat of sun
Others devoured by wild beasts
Exhausted and weary in the desert
Hearts broken, bodies shatter
Dazzled by beams of light who people the ninth heaven
Thousands of suns gather together
Outshine one another
What is the object of desire for the bird, the wren
The crow
The hoopoe we can't stop speaking of
Where is the trade abode beyond language
There was one alone, thy side, and one any one
The reality of the One and the reality of Thou
One tended to get holy but usually in a blood sacrifice
I, the scribe, the rabbit, the microscope
My sunlike Majesty is a mirror if you come as thirst,
as you experience that in mirror I said ripping down my various faces
A shadow is lost in the sun outside logic, which is a circle of hunger
The cycle of the recitals will also end by exodus of the known world
An escape beyond objects & categories
The revenge of Absalom for rape of his sister, Tamar,
And his subsequent death & she "desolate in her brother's house"
The patriarchal still among us full and growing, the sinisterarians
women abused, the endless show
Or Mayan gentility
Chacmool waiting for a resident votive
The look I know is the same of me,

overflowing terrestrial heart, looking out always, and waiting
and trying to move outside cosmic space
The birds are given a mysterious scroll and are told
to follow and fly with it to the end . . .
It is similar to the document the captain gave his crew, World War II
Leaving Burma for Japan
Here is the mystical emperor
could not help himself
You have heard of the demiurge
born and raised that way
and could not help the merging
The sounds of earth & sky in the grain
A meditation outside how your body looks
got stuck in growing and didn't stop wars, such the world
when you were born on D-Day
French & English lack words to interpret Kabuki, and translate
abstract Persian nouns
and the scissors to crack the codices
Or to see the divinity as mirror
Note the mention in Zosimus of Pano
Of a mirror made of electrums
And I thought watching the Polis, the POTUS
how mean we have been to our comrades
Those next door,
There is a dervish moon tonight
embrace turning as a stranger might enter a cave
on being captive
and we started to walk out to see a release for women
something could end outside of cosmic space
A world beheld in new freedoms not votes the same old jail,
same old death trap, as you woke screaming
what do you know of mystical epoch, caged age?
When we will come to account, in a cage?
Hirraz watched the fountain water rise, clear and crystal as ice

It leapt up to sprout like a tree, so there was
a generation force after all and Sheyla danced at that
and Hammuz sat before a bird and saw something
that resembled his old attire
shedding back the unaware cuff & boot
A creature of light, he tried to squawk as if warning
Nicodemus who held summits nine spheres
Waiting for the night hours as Nerval did
And there is Recital of Occidental Exile
a whole inventory of "moments"
Some for Nero here too, dumb with his fate
The planetary divinities are watching, nothing out of reach
And never reasonable to these bad actors, men of physic ruin
Hannappa asks a quest for the Orient
Sacrifices an eye to Shiva
Odin, northern, cold and there's Horus.
O amulet of Eye, lay down your spears, warless
Liverish moon, my treasure,
the wink of the mountain, her eye, we will
tempt to bare and unveil our love to all the eyes of
Nyx, Gaia, Sekhmet, Ishtar, Mahadevi, Kali, Ekajati
Logic, inside the temple where logic is the womb
as *Ta'wil* leads it back to string its meaning & truth
a one-eye kind of Angelology
In thereafter
But this written as an addition to our new techniques &
         systems taking hold to abandon the serotonin
as a way to not let these stories in poetry die
help, guide us, alphabets of night, and all the alphabets the world over
    all the thousands incarcerated
as we wait for our prisoners to come out, and own their release
and step our enlightenment up a bit
We'll keep wait, as fire dims

Voyant

Remnants of prophecy.
Speaking in tongues
Archaic forms
Who can understand possession? What voice orchestrated with
    the organs slung in the body?
Tell more of my Genesis, my ribs my sins, my telepathy
Tibetan Marpa, the translator, the traveler, helpmeet
Milarepa the poet, skin turns green from eating nettles in the cave
Enkidu, all the familiars in antithesis
Herminuisance the newest guide
our goddess Enheduanna, all the rage
in the (Mesopotopic) renaissance
Therigatha
Aztec
India
Bauls
Gassire, castanets
Maya: illusion is dance
Nine shaman songs of woe's men, Eurasian steppes
Ainu to shift
Arabic of accent
Uighur

And now also, is dirge, archival, what we love lives inside vaults
    and waves beg for evanescence. a particular destruction locked
    in the prophecy
Start over:
It would be the hermit and the dove. It would include the
    nuclear option under scrutiny
The sects & pacts of great ones broken, struck, ebbing.
It was to have been a compendium to perform with you, in
    your ear, in your chariot, a nearby vehicle.

It was supposed to have been trumpeted from the earliest
   time, names, scale of tribes, discoveries of first touch bone
   instruments, rattles of teeth, the runes on maps to find a
   psyche's way back. And as he divined the entheogen I know
   I had been there before. In the mud, in the long string of the
   lithe creatures, helping a child grow. Apotheosis.
It would rise to structure, maybe by joining hands and singing in
   a circle-round, vast in temple ceremony & cavern.
Then desires of song chant in obedience to the forms of spirit.
   What are they? They were supposed to help us guide me to you
   to be not the dactyls & spondees of war cry, not the blood on
   the shield
Facing your own mirror: lament the master plan, smash it, a
   generative zone heard the same wistful rift. Break now.
It was supposed to be a bundle of sticks gathered one at a time or
   when you might need fire
Antediluvian energies
Subterranean, study old maps of empire.
It has to have been a litany, who sang it? the cradle & birth of
   civilization.
Bhakti saints
Sumerian, Ugaritic, Hittite persons
Pre-Christian anthologies of struggle trying to make the case
Did they know anything outside war.
What was it?
[Ancient and primal seer in the cosmos speaks thus]

Come After

for Kora and Luna Luz

As I went down in the rivers to pray
Studying about that good old way
And who shall wear the robe and crown
Good Lord, show me the way!
O children, let's go down
Let's go down, come on down
Come on, children, let's go down
Down in the rivers to pray
                    —Traditional, variation

a yard is waiting for you
it's somewhat spare good-size yard
a variant of rubble
it was never a garden
it is waiting for you
to walk and crawl and lie on the ground
and maybe it will soon be a garden when
you come stand, bend, plant flowers
have a vegetable patch
helps feed you and
stems beginning to
feed others, dig down
study deeper
and play with a hose
will water come in pellets,
world given over
to simply horizontal barrier?
a virtual wall, an invisible wolf
will it rain and snow ever again?
and maybe, willful, have
a stream found virtuous as

water as occasion in a storm, to drink
and you be as most kids ask again
touch water, a waterfall and walking
this yard in a moist morning
and waits for you to come soon

YEAR OF THE WOOD SNAKE
~Sarva Mangalam~

Bibliography

Akash, Munir, and Carolyn Forché, trans. *Unfortunately, It Was Paradise: Selected Poems*. By Mahmoud Darwish. University of California Press, 2013.

Alexander, Will. *The Sri Lankan Loxodrome*. New Directions, 2009.

Ashbery, John. *Flow Chart*. Farrar, Straus & Giroux, 1998.

Baldwin, James. *The Fire Next Time*. Dial Press, 1963.

Barsamian, David, et al. *Targeting Iran*. City Lights Books, 2007.

Berssenbrugge, Mei-mei. *A Treatise on Stars*. New Directions, 2020.

Briffault, Herma, trans. *The Devastation of the Indies: A Brief Account*. By Bartolomé de Las Casas. Johns Hopkins University Press, 1992.

Burroughs, William S. *Nova Express*. Grove Press, 1964.

Burroughs, William S. *The Soft Machine*. Olympia Press, 1961.

Burroughs, William S. *The Ticket That Exploded*. Olympia Press, 1962.

Carroll, Robert P., and Stephen Prickett, eds. *The Bible: Authorized King James Version*. Oxford University Press, 1998.

Cohen, Mark E. *New Treasures of Sumerian Literature: "When the Moon Fell from the Sky" and Other Works*. CDL Press, 2017.

de Chirico, Giorgio. *Hebdomeros*. Peter Owen Ltd., 1929.

Dylan, Bob. "Murder Most Foul." *Rough and Rowdy Ways*. Columbia Records, 2020.

Edwards, Kari. *Obedience*. Factory School, 2005.

Eubanks, Ivan, and Kareem James Abu-Zeid, trans. *Songs of Mihyar the Damascene*. By Adonis. New Directions, 2019.

Fast Speaking Music and Laurel Road Studios. *Astral Omens*, 2024.

"Human Rights Watch: Israel Has Tortured Detained Palestinian Medical Workers." *Democracy Now!*, August 26, 2024.

Jarnot, Isaac, trans. *Iliad. Book XXII: The Death of Hector*. By Homer. Book*hug Press, 2007.

Khalidi, Rashid. *The Hundred Years' War on Palestine*. Metropolitan Books, 2020.

Kongtrül, Jamgön. *Myriad Worlds*. Snow Lion Publications, 1993.

Kramer, Samuel Noah. *The Sumerians*. University of Chicago Press, 1963.

Lippard, Lucy R. *Overlay: Contemporary Art and the Art of Prehistory*. New Press, 1983.

Mbembe, Achille. *Brutalism*. Duke University Press, 2024.

Mercer, Samuel. *The Pyramid Texts*. Forgotten Books, 2008.

Merwin, W. S. *The Mays of Ventadorn*. National Geographic Society, 2002.

Öcalan, Abdullah. *Beyond State, Power, and Violence*. PM Press, 2022.

Petrarca, Francesco, and Bruce Rogers. *Fifteen Sonnets of Petrarch*. Houghton Mifflin, 1903.

Paden, William D., ed. *The Voice of the Trobairitz: Perspectives on the Women Troubadours*. University of Pennsylvania Press, 1989.

Petti, Alessandro, Sandi Hilal, and Eyal Weizman. *Architecture after Revolution*. Sternberg Press, 2013.

Powers, Thomas, "Who Won the Cold War?" *The New York Review of Books*, June 1996.

Virey, Philippe, trans. "The Precepts of Ptah-hotep." By Ptah-hotep. In A. H. Sayce, ed. *Records of the Past*, vol. 3. Samuel Bagster and Sons, Ltd., 1888.

Pusey, Edward Bouverie, trans. *The Confessions of Saint Augustine*. By Saint Augustine. Random House Publishing Group, 2000.

Sargeant, Jack. *Naked Lens: Beat Cinema*. Soft Skull Press, 2008.

Scalapino, Leslie. *It's Go in Horizontal*. University of California Press, 2008.

Stein, Charles. "The Position of Parmenides," Charles Stein Poet, accessed March 20, 2025, charlessteinpoet.com.

Tanahashi, Kazuaki, ed. *Moon in a Dewdrop: Writings of Zen Master Dōgen*. By Dōgen. North Point Press, 2000.

Townsend, Camilla. *Fifth Sun: A New History of the Aztecs*. Oxford University Press, 2019.

Tugendhaft, Aaron. *The Idols of ISIS: From Assyria to the Internet*. University of Chicago Press, 2021.

Tsvetaeva, Marina. *Earthly Signs: Moscow Diaries, 1917–1922*. Yale University Press, 2002.

Vajravairochana Translation Committee, eds. *The Sadhana of Mahamudra*. Nālandā Translation Committee, 1990.

Visuals

Collage details from "Wind Up Doll" by John Ashbery, used by permission of the estate of John Ashbery. With thanks to the Tibor de Nagy Gallery.

Photo, "Detail from 'Scenes from the Life of Christ' by Giotto di Bondone" by the author, 2020.

Photo, "The Great Stupa of Dharmakaya" by Zoe Brezsny, 2024.

Photo collage, "Hierve el Agua, Oaxaca" by the author, 2020.

Images of work by Kiki Smith, used by permission of Kiki Smith, and Universal Limited Arts Editions. With thanks to the Pace Gallery and the exhibit "Murmur," 2019.

Mushroom image accompanying "Sorcery: Times of the Chthonic" by LukaGift/Shutterstock.com

Photo, "Cinéma vérité from Mimi Gross studio," by Zoe Brezsny, 2025.

Image of work by Mimi Gross, used by permission of Mimi Gross.

Printing block images accompanying "Extinction Aria," used by permission of David Sellers, publisher, printer, designer of Pied Oxen Press.

Anne Waldman, poet, founder, performer, activist, professor, is the author and editor of numerous volumes of poetry and literary anthologies. *The Iovis Trilogy: Colors in the Mechanism of Concealment* (Coffee House Press), a thousand-page epic, won the PEN Center Award for Poetry. Penguin has published her books over many years, including *Marriage: A Sentence*, *Manatee/Humanity*, and *Trickster Feminism*, among others. Her album *SCIAMACHY* was released in 2020 by Fast Speaking Music and has been described by Patti Smith as "exquisitely potent, a psychic shield for our times." Waldman was one of the original founders and workers at the Poetry Project at St. Mark's Church in-the-Bowery in 1966, becoming director in 1968 and also founder of the historic New Year's Day Marathon that continues to flourish unabated.

She also went on to cofound the Jack Kerouac School of Disembodied Poetics program at Naropa University, developing its MFA program and continuing the celebrated Summer Writing Program, which has welcomed thousands into its generative mandala in Boulder since 1974. She has recently curated events for Giorno Poetry Systems; the "Beat Art Work: Power of the Gaze" exhibit, celebrating visual work of the Beat literary generation; and the Outsider Art Fair in New York City in 2024. And cocurator of *The Video Work of Ed Bowes: Language and Light*, Anthology Film Archives, 2024.

She was arrested at Rocky Flats with Daniel Ellsberg and Allen Ginsberg in the 1970s, reading poems that challenged deliveries of plutonium for the manufacturing of pits for nuclear warheads. She was part of protests during the Vietnam War and at the Chicago Seven trial, and has participated in countercultural interventions in subsequent times, such as Occupy Wall Street, the Women's March, George Floyd protests, and, right now, protests against the slaughter in Palestine and anti-Semitism in the US. She has organized events with Ammiel Alcalay under the rubric Poetry Is News. She also works with the expanding Rizoma collective of musicians, artists, and poets in Mexico City.

Waldman was a keynote speaker for the Jaipur Literature Festival in India as well as the "Bob Dylan and the Beats" conference in Tulsa in the spring of 2022, and she wrote the libretto for the critically acclaimed and Grammy-nominated opera/movie *Black Lodge* (with music by composer David T. Little), which premiered at Opera Philadelphia in October 2022. Waldman has collaborated with many artists, filmmakers, dancers, and musicians, including filmmaker Ed Bowes, painter Pat Steir, artist Richard Tuttle, composer and performer Meredith Monk, choreographer Douglas Dunn, and saxophonist James Brandon Lewis. *Outrider*, a documentary directed by Alystyre Julian with and about Anne Waldman (produced by Sarah Riggs, with executive producer Martin Scorsese), was released in 2025. Waldman is most recently the author of *Archivist Scissors* (Staircase Books, 2025); *The Velvet Wire* with No Land (Granary Books, 2024); *Bard, Kinetic* (Coffee House Press, 2023), a memoir in prose and poetry; and coeditor with Emma Gomis of *New Weathers: Poetics from the Naropa Archive* (Nightboat, 2022). *Publishers Weekly* has called Anne Waldman a "countercultural giant." From the Poetry Foundation (Chicago) review of Waldman's *Bard, Kinetic*: "Waldman is one of the most important and irreducible living American poets."

annewaldman.org

GAROUS
ABDOLMALEKIAN
Lean Against This Late Hour

PAIGE ACKERSON-KIELY
Dolefully, A Rampart Stands

JOHN ASHBERY
Selected Poems
Self-Portrait in a Convex Mirror

PAUL BEATTY
Joker, Joker, Deuce

JOSHUA BENNETT
Owed
The Sobbing School
The Study of Human Life

TED BERRIGAN
The Sonnets

LAUREN BERRY
The Lifting Dress

JOE BONOMO
Installations

PHILIP BOOTH
Lifelines: Selected Poems
  1950–1999
Selves

JIM CARROLL
Fear of Dreaming:
  The Selected Poems
Living at the Movies
Void of Course

SU CHO
The Symmetry of Fish

ADRIENNE CHUNG
Organs of Little Importance

RIO CORTEZ
Golden Ax

MARISSA DAVIS
End of Empire

ALISON HAWTHORNE
DEMING
Genius Loci
Rope
Stairway to Heaven

CARL DENNIS
Another Reason
Callings
Earthborn
New and Selected Poems
  1974–2004
Night School
Practical Gods
Ranking the Wishes
Unknown Friends

DIANE DI PRIMA
Loba

STUART DISCHELL
Backwards Days
Dig Safe

STEPHEN DOBYNS
Velocities: New and Selected
  Poems 1966–1992

EDWARD DORN
Way More West

HEID E. ERDRICH
Little Big Bully

ROGER FANNING
The Middle Ages

ADAM FOULDS
The Broken Word: An Epic
  Poem of the British Empire
  in Kenya, and the Mau Mau
  Uprising Against It

CARRIE FOUNTAIN
Burn Lake
Instant Winner
The Life

AMY GERSTLER
Dearest Creature
Ghost Girl
Index of Women
Is This My Final Form?
Medicine
Nerve Storm
Scattered at Sea

EUGENE GLORIA
Drivers at the Short-Time Motel
Hoodlum Birds
My Favorite Warlord
Sightseer in This Killing City

DEBORA GREGER
In Darwin's Room

ZEINA HASHEM BECK
O

TERRANCE HAYES
American Sonnets for My Past
  and Future Assassin
Hip Logic
How to Be Drawn
Lighthead
So to Speak
Wind in a Box

NATHAN HOKS
The Narrow Circle

ROBERT HUNTER
Sentinel and Other Poems

MARY KARR
Viper Rum

W. B. KECKLER
Sanskrit of the Body

JACK KEROUAC
Book of Blues
Book of Haikus
Book of Sketches

JOANNA KLINK
Circadian
Excerpts from a
  Secret Prophecy
The Nightfields
Raptus

JOANNE KYGER
As Ever: Selected Poems

ANN LAUTERBACH
Door
Hum
If in Time: Selected Poems
  1975–2000
On a Stair
Or to Begin Again
Spell
Under the Sign

CORINNE LEE
Plenty
Pyx

PHILLIS LEVIN
May Day
Mr. Memory & Other Poems

PATRICIA LOCKWOOD
Motherland Fatherland
  Homelandsexuals

WILLIAM LOGAN
Rift of Light

J. MICHAEL MARTINEZ
Museum of the Americas
Tarta Americana

ADRIAN MATEJKA
The Big Smoke
Map to the Stars
Mixology
Somebody Else Sold the World

AMBER McBRIDE
Thick with Trouble

MICHAEL McCLURE
Huge Dreams: San Francisco
  and Beat Poems

ROSE McLARNEY
Colorfast
Forage
Its Day Being Gone

DAVID MELTZER
David's Copy:
  The Selected Poems of
  David Meltzer

TERESA K. MILLER
Borderline Fortune

ROBERT MORGAN
Dark Energy
Terroir

CAROL MUSKE-DUKES
Blue Rose
An Octave Above Thunder:
  New and Selected Poems
Red Trousseau
Twin Cities

ALICE NOTLEY
Being Reflected Upon
Certain Magical Acts
Culture of One
The Descent of Alette
Disobedience
For the Ride
In the Pines
Mysteries of Small Houses

WILLIE PERDOMO
The Crazy Bunch
The Essential Hits of
  Shorty Bon Bon

DANIEL POPPICK
Fear of Description

LIA PURPURA
It Shouldn't Have Been
  Beautiful

LAWRENCE RAAB
The History of Forgetting
Visible Signs:
  New and Selected Poems

BARBARA RAS
The Last Skin
One Hidden Stuff

M.S. REDCHERRIES
mother

MICHAEL ROBBINS
Alien vs. Predator
The Second Sex
Walkman

PATTIANN ROGERS
Flickering
Generations
Holy Heathen Rhapsody
Quickening Fields
Wayfare

SAM SAX
Madness

ROBYN SCHIFF
Information Desk: An Epic
A Woman of Property

WILLIAM STOBB
Absentia
Nervous Systems

TRYFON TOLIDES
An Almost Pure Empty Walking

VINCENT TORO
Hivestruck
Tertulia

PAUL TRAN
All the Flowers Kneeling

SARAH VAP
Viability

ANNE WALDMAN
Gossamurmur
Kill or Cure
Manatee/Humanity
Mesopotopia
Trickster Feminism

JAMES WELCH
Riding the Earthboy 40

PHILIP WHALEN
Overtime: Selected Poems

PHILLIP B. WILLIAMS
Mutiny

MIA S. WILLIS
the space between men

ROBERT WRIGLEY
Anatomy of Melancholy and
  Other Poems
Beautiful Country
Box
Earthly Meditations:
  New and Selected Poems
Lives of the Animals
Reign of Snakes
The True Account of Myself
  as a Bird

MARK YAKICH
The Importance of Peeling
  Potatoes in Ukraine
Spiritual Exercises
Unrelated Individuals Forming
  a Group Waiting to Cross